Student Workbook
for
The Art of Editing
in the Age of Convergence

Student Workbook
for
The Art of Editing
in the Age of Convergence

Ninth Edition

Brian S. Brooks
Missouri School of Journalism

James L. Pinson
Eastern Michigan University

PEARSON

Boston   New York   San Francisco
Mexico City   Montreal   Toronto   London   Madrid   Munich   Paris
Hong Kong   Singapore   Tokyo   Cape Town   Sydney

ISBN-13: 978-0-205-56966-3
ISBN-10:   0-205-56966-8

Printed in the United States of America

10 9 8 7 6 5 4 3 2 1   12 11 10 09 08

Contents

Preface

The third edition of *The Art of Editing* was the first to be accompanied by a workbook of exercises. The overwhelming success of that workbook is evidence that many teachers nationwide shared our concerns about spending too many hours preparing exercises at the expense of more productive teaching activity. The availability of workbook exercises helps to solve that problem.

This updated version of the workbook gives teachers access to exercises that have been tried and tested by students at the Missouri School of Journalism and at Eastern Michigan University. Collectively, the exercises cover almost every point of editing that could be made in an editing class. We believe they nicely complement the extensively revised text.

We have prepared the exercises with both the teacher and student in mind. Instructions are specific when necessary but deliberately open-ended when, in our opinion, there is need for the teacher to guide the students closely. For example, teachers may choose to alter or supplement the instructions for layout and design exercises; no two teachers approach the subject alike.

The workbook is divided into sections that correspond to the major blocks of instruction in the textbook. In almost every section, there are quizzes, problems and exercises for students to tackle.

The order in which the exercises appear reflects the manner in which most teachers approach the introductory copy-editing course. However, those who prefer to begin with headline writing or some other subject will find it easy to skip back and forth as they find necessary.

A few words about the appendixes are in order. Appendix I is a handy reference for those who cannot remember copy-editing symbols when they first begin editing. Appendix II is a headline schedule for those who choose to use it; some teachers may prefer to use their own, and some may choose to use none at all and rely on computers to count headlines. Increasingly, computers are replacing manual methods of headline counting in the classroom, just as they have in newsrooms.

Appendixes III and IV are helpful in teaching students to check verifiable information: the spellings of names, the accuracy of addresses and similar items. Appendix V is a guide to layout and design, but again, some teachers may prefer a different approach.

This workbook is intended as a complement to the Ninth Edition of *The Art of Editing*. Despite that, either the workbook or the textbook can be used alone by teachers who prefer a different approach.

We hope this workbook will help many teachers find the time to give more individual attention to students by relieving them of the burden of preparing exercises. It has done so for us. We also hope it helps students learn the fundamentals of copy editing by giving them an abundance of carefully constructed exercises on which to work. It has done so for our students, who deserve much of the credit for field-testing the exercises. We are indebted to them.

Brian S. Brooks
Columbia, Missouri

James L. Pinson
Ypsilanti, Michigan

1

Editing for Today's Changing Media

Student Name _____ Course _____ Date_____

QUIZ: EDITING FOR TODAY'S CHANGING MEDIA
Circle T for true or F for false.

T F   1. Editors traditionally have functioned as gatekeepers, but that function is fading as news consumers have more and more ways of receiving information.

T F   2. Editors of today are probably more powerful than those of the past.

T F   3. Many editors bemoan the decline in readership of news readers need.

T F   4. Agenda-setting is a function of editors that is increasing in importance.

T F   5. Producing journalism based on truth and accuracy is the best way to earn the public's trust.

T F   6. Newspaper circulation remains almost flat as the population continues to grow.

T F   7. The increase in the number of cable television channels has not hurt the major broadcast networks, which remain extremely powerful.

T F   8. Radio audiences are as large as those of newspapers and television combined.

T F   9. Magazines are a poor vehicle for targeted marketing and advertising.

T F   10. Newspapers of today are only marginally profitable.

T F   11. Magazines often have appealing audiences for advertisers who target them.

T F   12. Media convergence is a fading trend.

T F   13. Television news standards are generally considered to be more demanding than those of the print media.

T F   14. The Federal Communications Commission has proposed rules that would relax standards on common ownership of newspapers and television stations.

T F   15. It would be rare for a print reporter to be asked to get sound bites for the paper's Web site because of union restrictions.

T F   16. Conflict is often considered one of the primary factors in determining news value.

T F   17. Prominent people make news more interesting.

T F   18. The Internet seldom offers people information they cannot find in the traditional media.

T F   19. Larry King's television show is a news program.

T F   20. People skilled as editors are not in high demand.

Student Name _____ Course _____ Date_____

PROBLEMS: EDITING FOR TODAY'S CHANGING MEDIA

1. Describe in your own words the impact of the developing new media systems on more traditional media outlets such as newspapers, magazines, radio and television.

2. Explain which of the existing media are best-positioned to take advantage of the explosion of new media technologies. Why?

2

The Editor
and the Audience

QUIZ: THE EDITOR AND THE AUDIENCE
Circle T for true or F for false.

T F   1. Editors and their audiences usually function in harmony.

T F   2. The percentage of American adults reading newspapers is steadily declining.

T F   3. As older newspaper readers die, young ones are taking their place.

T F   4. Younger readers are more likely to consume information on the Internet.

T F   5. Audience fragmentation is a serious problem for the media, and it is a phenomenon fed by advertisers' desire to reach target audiences.

T F   6. Focus groups of readers are an important way for editors to attempt to understand what readers want.

T F   7. Redesign projects at newspapers often are launched as a result of declining circulation.

T F   8. Newspapers must pander to readers to remain viable.

T F   9. Readers do not want to interact with reporters.

T F   10. Many newspaper web sites are mere regurgitations of the print product.

T F   11. Most Americans report that television is their main source of news.

T F   12. Internet advertising revenue far exceeds that of television and newspapers combined.

T F   13. Many view the Internet as the medium of the future.

T F   14. Readers are not interested in hard news and instead prefer features.

T F   15. Overall, readers like their newspapers.

T F   16. Public journalism is pandering to the needs of public officials.

T F   17. Factual and spelling errors do little to erode confidence in newspapers.

T F   18. Members of the public who have actually encountered reporters are the most critical of the news media.

T F   19. Many news consumers believe the concept of journalistic ethics is an oxymoron.

T F   20. Readers needs change, and editors need to keep up.

Student Name _____ Course _____ Date_____

PROBLEMS: THE EDITOR AND THE AUDIENCE

1. Describe the major findings of the latest research on newspaper readership. Describe how you, as an editor, would attempt to solve the problems posed by the results of those studies.

2. Discuss the relationship of newspapers, television and other competing media. List the ways in which they complement each other as well as compete.

3

The Editing Process

Student Name _____ Course _____ Date_____

QUIZ: THE EDITING PROCESS
Circle T for true or F for false.

T F 1. Because it's harder to hire good copy editors than good reporters, copy editors can often go faster to a better paper than reporters can.

T F 2. Reporters generally know the 10 percent of style rules that are used 90 percent of the time, so at a professional newspaper, many of their style mistakes will be the ones that are 90 percent of the stylebook but used only 10 percent of the time.

T F 3. If you're a copy-editing intern and spot major changes you'd like to make in a story, go ahead and rewrite it because that's your job.

T F 4. One way to develop your skills as an editor is to keep note cards about things you have to look up.

T F 5. The person in charge of the newsroom at a paper is typically the general manager.

T F 6. The city editor edits a story mainly for details like grammar, usage and style.

T F 7. The rim editor assigns stories for a slot person to edit and write headlines.

T F 8. On the sports desk and lifestyle desk, the assignment editor may also act as slot and rim editor.

T F 9. Macro and micro, "The Seven C's Plus One" and "The Three R's" are different ways to summarize the things that editors do.

T F 10. Making writing "reader-centered" means giving the readers what they need and want and making it new for them.

T F 11. Making writing "readable" just means to make sure the subjects are interesting.

T F 12. "The Three R's of Editing" are to make sure the story is right, right, right.

T F 13. There's no upper limit to how high you should pump up in the "intensity density" in a publication.

T F 14. Copy editors are often expected to edit and write a headline for about one story every 15 minutes.

T F 15. If you're having trouble getting a headline to fit, it's typically OK just to go ahead and change the size of the type without bothering the slot person.

T F 16. To abbreviate a word, circle it.

T F 17. To delete a letter at the end of a word on hard copy, draw a diagonal line through the letter, then put a loop both over the top and under the bottom.

T F 18. Proofreading is the same as copy editing done one extra time.

T F 19. When reading a proof, mark the mistakes in the margin instead of in the copy itself.

T F 20. If a story is too long, you can cut the exact number of lines needed to fit or up to three extra typically.

EXERCISE: WOULD YOU BE HAPPIER AS A REPORTER OR COPY EDITOR?

Most students in journalism have never considered a career in copy editing until they take an editing class. Most have simply been unaware of it as an option. This is a self-scoring quiz meant to help you determine whether reporting or copy editing would be a better match for you. Circle the letter of the statement in each pair that best fits you, then check your results.

Most students in journalism have never considered a career in copy editing until they take an editing class. Most have simply been unaware of it as an option. This is a self-scoring quiz meant to help you determine whether reporting or copy editing would be a better match for you. Circle the letter of the statement in each pair that best fits you, then check your results on the back of this page.

1. Growing up, I was more interested
   A.   in socializing with other kids
   B.   reading

2. I would prefer spending my workday
   A.   talking and listening to people
   B.   alone with my work but in the company of friends I know

3. In dealing with other people
   A.   I can easily put stressful situations behind me and so don't mind them much.
   B.   I don't like stressful situations so prefer to avoid them.

4. The hardest part of reporting for me is
   A.   writing
   B.   interviewing

5. If the writing process is seen as three stages – 1) coming up with ideas and gathering information, 2) writing and 3) revising – the part I enjoy the most other than writing is
   A.   coming up with ideas and gathering information
   B.   revising

6. In journalism classes, my attitude about learning grammar and style could be better described as
   A.   it's mainly a waste of time and boring
   B.   it's an important part of my training and interesting

7. Writing headlines and laying out pages – designing how they look --
    A.   are fun for me but not so much as writing a story
    B.   are as much fun for me as writing a story

8. I would prefer to work in a job that gave me variety through
    A.   meeting new people
    B.   dealing with a variety of topics and job tasks

9. Seeing my name in print each day in a byline is
    A.   very important to me
    B.   not that important to me

10. When I go home after work
    A.   it doesn't matter to me if I have to devote free time to the job.
    B.   it's important to me to be able to put the job aside and feel done for the day

WHAT YOUR SCORE MEANS
Count the number of B's.
8-10 B's -- You should strongly consider a career in copy editing. You would probably enjoy it more than reporting.
4-7 B's --You could probably enjoy either reporting or copy editing. If you hadn't considered copy editing as a career before, add it to your options.
0-3 B's -- Although copy editing doesn't seem like a good fit for you right now, you will still benefit from this course by learning why editors change your copy and how you can stop some of that by making the fixes first yourself.

EXERCISE: COPY-EDITING SYMBOLS
Edit these sentences using the proper copy-editing symbols (see Appendix I).

1. She lives at 1926 West Boulevard South in Springfield.

2. One of the biggest movie hits of all time was "Casablanca."

3. Newspapers mail copies with special second class postage rates.

4. It was so hot the city used 123,000 gallons of water.

5. The Springfield Mayor sent the City Manager to Keokuk, Iowa for the meeting.

6. Any top rated performer could draw a big crowd there.

7. She said six thousand people could not get into the arena.

8. Sergeant First Class Anna Lopez was in charge of the platoon.

9. Annettes brother was the Number One-ranked heavywieght contender.

10. We are eager to help nations in need," the president said.

11. Workers toiled through the night to rescue those in the mine.

12. The Atlanta braves are chall enging for the Eastern Division title.

13. 'Tkae a hike!," he shouted in anger.

14. The best of the gymnasts was from the University of Nebraska.

15. The well known composer was born in Medford, Oregon, but moved to Los Angeles, CA, in 1991.

16. Peach trees are common in Georgia, and Magnolias often are associated with Mississippi.

17. Does the governor know, What happened in the senate today?

18. He arrived in Rome at 7 p.m. Tues. night.

19. The sherriff said all deputies would start carrying 38-caliber revolvers.

20. The Orioles Baltimore are leading the Amercan League East.

EXERCISE: COPY-EDITING SYMBOLS
Edit these sentences using the proper copy-editing symbols (see Appendix I).

1. "I hope this is the end of it, he said.

2. Ninety-eight percent of Spaniards claim to be Roman catholics.

3. Laguage skills are important to the journalist, the professor said.

4. Eagle Electric Company is on Eighth Street in Springfield.

5. New Yorkrs take such events in stride.

6. The last last time I saw you was in Columbia, S.c.

7. Military police arrested James E. Donatelli, 19 of 201 E. Cherry St.

8. Troops exchanged fire today along the border, military officials reported.

9. Graduation ceremonies have been scheuled for 3 pm Friday in Nogales.

10. "Then he said, 'Don't fire until you see the whites of their eyes."

11. Houston is one of the most humid cities in Tex.

12. It doesn't take long to drive from Washington D.C. to Baltimore.

13. "Luck has nothing do to with it," Marlow said.

14. The recieving deaprtment is in the rear of the store.

15. TV is a major source of entertainment for most americans, Katie Couric said.

16. "Why didn't he hit it to right field?" the sportswriter asked.

17. Is America facing another guns-or-butter dilemma?

18. He starred on 'Father Knows Best' during the 1,950's.

19. "The Electric Co." is a popular T.V. show for youngsters.

20. Col. Robert Lopez was 8th in his class at the US Air Force Academy.

EXERCISE: PROOFREADING SYMBOLS
Correct these stories using the proper proofreading symbols (see Appendix I).

A Tuesday evening fire in Harrisburg is a reminder to keep flus from fireplaces and wood-burning stoves inspected and cleaned periodically.

Assistant Chief Ken Hines of the Springfield County Fire Protection District said a creosote buildup in the chimney flu ignited a blaze in the home of Gary and Patty Long.

Fire fighters who arrived on the scene about 9:45 p.m. saw fire and smoke on the outside of the home. The fire had been burning inside for several hours but had not been visible. It took three hours for firefighters to extinguish the fire. Hines said there was about $15,000 in damage to the house and its contents. No onne was injured.

The National Fire Protection Association says home heating is the second leading cause of home fires in the U. S. Owners of wood-stoves and fireplaces need to have their chimneys and flus inspected at the beginning of every heating season and cleaned if necessary. When wood burns, creosote builds up in chimneys and can cause chimney fires if not properly cleaned. To minimize the build-up, stove owners should burn only good, seasoned wood, Hines said.

Springield fire fighters responding to a gas leak Wednesday after noon stopped traffic for about 20 minutes at W. Ash St. and Garth Avenue.

Union Electric Co. workers shut off the line and stopped the leak about 1:40 p.m. while fire department officials cleared traffic as a precautionary measure. No injuries were reported.

The leak was causerd when a backhoe, digging a hole for a water line, tapped into a 1-inch plastic gass line. The property is currently under construction by Advance Builders, a Springfield-based construction company.

"It's not uncommmon for an excavation to hit into gas liens," said Dan Hale of Advance Builders. "Of course, sometimes when you're running a machine like that, you mis judge and go an inch or so deeper."

Harold Hackman, a spokesman for Union Electric, the company that provides gas service for Springfield, said: "There was quite a bit of gas in the air. We were there with in 10 minutes."

Student Name _____ Course _____ Date_____

EXERCISE: PROOFREADING SYMBOLS
Correct these stories using the proper proofreading symbols (see Appendix I).

A state social worker and an image consultant were arrested Sunday after police found 25 pouunds of marijuana in their Springfield home.

Robert L. Drexler, 27, owner of Miller Ltd., and Rebeccca Dillon, 22, who works for the Division of Family Services, 405 N. Ninth St., were arr ested on suspicion of possession of mairjuana with the intent to distribute and sale of a controlled substance, police said.

The charges were reduced to possession of a controlled subbstance of more than 35 grams, said Dan Viets, Dillon's attorney.

One pound of dried marijuana would fill a grocery sack, and is worth between $500 and 1,500, Springfield Police Capt. Chris Egbert said.

"Compared to many seizures on the highway, this is not a very large amount. But for Springfield, it is, Viets said.

Drexler and Dillon were arraigned Monday in Springfield Co. Circuit Court and later released from Boone County Jail.

Two burglars apparently in search of money broke into an emergency food distribution center early Tuesday but they didn't get so much as a can of beans.

The vandals cut a back-door padlock and entered Ann Carlson's Emergency Food Pantry, Inc., at about 3 a.m. ``I imagine they were looking for money, but we don't keep any money here," said Mike Bequette, a member of the pantry's board of directors.

Once the vandals got inside, they tried to torch the front of a soda machine by lighting the spray from a can of WD-40 that was laying near the machine, Bequette said.

The men took two fire extinguishers from the pantry and coated the inside of the building with a dry chemical extinguishing powder. They also draged a fireproof file cabinet into the parking lot and damaged it.

A snowplow driver saw a truck and at least one person in the parking lot of the pantry at 1408 Indiana Ave., but the driver thought the truck was cleaning off the parking lot, Bequette said.

The only thing unaccounted for was one of the fire extinguishers.

Capt. Dennis Veach of the Springfield Police Dept. believes the burglars intended to rob the pantry because of the vandalized cabinet and soda machine.

Student Name _____ Course _____ Date_____

PROBLEMS: THE EDITING PROCESS

1. Describe in your own words the duties and responsibilities of an editor at a typical newspaper, magazine, radio and television station. How do their roles differ?

2. List the titles of the five top-ranking editors of your local newspaper. Briefly describe the duties of each.

4

Macro Editing
for the Big Picture

QUIZ: MACRO EDITING FOR THE BIG PICTURE
Circle T for true or F for false.

T F   1. "Macro editing" refers to editing with an eye toward details.

T F   2. The best lead is how the story could affect the readers, the next best is what would most interest the readers, and the fallback position is to make sure that the story at least focuses on people.

T F   3. When considering how long a story should run, consider only the story itself, not other news in the newspaper or broadcast.

T F   4. All other things being equal, a copy desk would normally cut local stories before wire ones because the wire stories are required to run in full.

T F   5. Hard-news stories typically have a bottom-line lead and an inverted-pyramid structure.

T F   6. A hard-news story should never have a feature-style lead.

T F   7. If the who in a hard-news story is not well-known to your audience, a delayed lead should be used, typically with the person's name at the start of the second paragraph.

T F   8. Journalists write about events in place, day, time order.

T F   9. Use the day of the week in describing something that happened within a week forward or backward or publication. Use the date for something more than a week in the past or future.

T F 10. The "bottom line" appears in a feature story but several paragraphs down instead of in the lead.

T F 11. Every feature story needs a news peg.

T F 12. Feature stories are normally written in past tense, hard-news stories in present tense.

T F 13. Feature stories should be tightened from the middle, not cut from the end.

T F 14. One of the best ways to start a soft-news story is with a dictionary definition.

T F 15. It's important to get all of the Five W's and an H – who, what, when, where, why and how – in the lead.

T F 16. The "seesaw technique" is to alternate between statements presenting information and quotations that back them.

T F 17. An editor should make sure a story doesn't leave any unanswered questions – partly because readers are confused if there are and partly because readers expect more details in the newspaper than in broadcast news.

T F 18. Editors should check stories for inconsistencies not only within the story but also with previous stories or other information they've encountered.

T F 19. George Santayana said, "Those who ignore history are doomed to repeat it."

T F 20. When using information from press releases or the Internet, it's especially important not to trust biased sources.

T F 21. When a reporter gets word of a great-sounding story but with too few details to track down, it may be an example of an "urban legend."

T F 22. The safest policy is not to "doctor" quotes.

B. Put the letter of the best answer in front of the number.

____ 23. The typical order of items in a hard-news lead is which of the following? Optional items are in parentheses.)
a. who, what (time, day and place)
b. who, what, where, when (how and why)
c. what, who, where and when
d. when, where, who and what

____ 24. Which of the following best summarizes a couple of the ways that editors introduce errors into stories?
a. trusting the reporter and not looking things up
b. writing headlines, captions and blurbs and rewriting the story
c. spicing up the story and not caring whether it's true
d. injecting their own racist or political views

____ 25. The four main things journalists typically mean by being objective include all BUT which of the following?
a. sticking to facts
b. being neutral
c. being fair
d. being politically correct

EXERCISE: LEADS

A. Put a check in front of the people who would probably receive an immediate ID lead in a hard-news story in the *Kansas City* (Mo.) *Star.*

1.___Brad Pitt
2.___the governor of Missouri
3.___the governor of West Virginia
4.___the secretary of state of Missouri
5.___the mayor of Kansas City
6.___the mayor of Boise, Idaho
7.___a member of the City Council
8.___a burglary victim
9.___an extortion suspect
10.___a professor at the University of Missouri-Kansas City

B. Circle the correct way in each pair to refer to an event happening on that day if today is Sunday, March 15, 2009.
11. last Thursday; March 12
12. next Wednesday; March 18
13. yesterday; Saturday
14. tonight; Sunday night
15. two weeks ago from this Wednesday; March 4

C. Edit the following hard-news leads, either fixing problems that need it or querying those that might require additional information.

1. In Dexter on Monday at 7 p.m., the City Council will meet.

2. Friday, Phyllis Henderson spoke about cancer research.

3. On Tuesday around 2 p.m., a robbery took place on the 1400 block of Maple St. when Ben Addams, a Springfield plumber making a house call, was threatened at gunpoint if he didn't turn over his wallet.

4. Bill Weston, who has a doctorate from the University of Southern California at Los Angeles and who has been a professor of plant pathology at the University of Missouri-Columbia since 1995, where he developed the Phillips plant smear in 1987, has done it again! He's developed a pollination pocket indicator.

5. The Springfield Fire Department answered a fire alarm at 1:15 a.m. Monday at the Sears store downtown at 1320 Main Street and found when they arrived that there had

33

been an arson at the business. The Fire Department arrived in 10 minutes after the call in three hook-and-ladder trucks, but the building was destroyed despite their heroic efforts.

6. In a dramatic move, Federal Reserve Chairman Ben Bernanke has announced the board is slashing interest rates another half a percent.

7. The government announced yesterday that the rate of inflation calculated on an annual basis had declined from 4.6 percent in December to 3.5 percent in January, while unemployment continued at a postwar high of 9.2 percent during the same month, with more than 890,000 people out of work.

8. Four weeks into its two-month fund-raising effort, the United Way of Springfiled said Wednesday it had raised $81,229 so far out of a campaign goal of $1.4 million, or only about 5.8 percent of its goal.

9. Have you ever wondered what paint in your house and the gasoline in your car used to have in common? The answer is lead -- and exposure to it has been found to produce learning disabilities in children and serious health problems in children and adults.

10. Success! What is success? "Achieving wealth or fame" is how Webster's dictionary defines success. But to Willy Stephens, it just means being able to feed himself again, something most of us take for granted.

Student Name _____ Course _____ Date_____

QUIZ: MACRO EDITING
UNANSWERED QUESTIONS, SAY-NOTHING QUOTATIONS, FLOW, ACCURACY

A. What questions do the following sentences raise about the story?

1. (LEAD) A large crowd showed up in Kansas City to hear President Bush speak Tuesday.

2 (LEAD) The Missouri Tigers lost their season opener Saturday.

3. (LEAD) An Eastern Michigan University professor died Monday afternoon while playing tennis on campus.

4. The last line of a story about a traffic accident is, "This is the ninth accident reported at that intersection in the past three months." Even without seeing the previous sentences in the story, what can you say the reporter has apparently missed?

B. What would you do with the following quotations?

5. "Teachers should not expect a raise this year because the district is in a zero-increase posture," said the school board president.

6. The coach says the main thing the team has to do is to stick to "fundamentals. We've got to play the kind of ball we know we're capable of playing. If we just take one game at a time and give 110 percent, I think we've got a shot this season", he said.

C. How could the following lines from stories be given better transitions or otherwise be improved?

7. In another related development today, the Michigan Legislature ...

8. Besides passing the anti-smoking ordinance just discussed, the City Council also overrode a Planning and Zoning Commission decision to rezone a property near the airport as "light industrial," tabled a proposal to consider removing parking meters from the downtown area, approved the widening of Main Street and censured the mayor for accepting money from the developer who had asked that the property near the airport be rezoned.

9. While the Democratic caucus met today, the Republicans met Thursday.

D. What's wrong with the following statement?

10. As Humphrey Bogart said in "Casablanca," "Play it again, Sam."

EXERCISE: FACT CHECKING

Use the World Wide Web or reference books to determine whether the following statements are true, and record your answer and source. The answers are not in the textbook. (Note: You may want to check more than one source, as you may find contradictory answers.)

THE PRESIDENCY

1. A genetic study in Nature magazine proved that only Thomas Jefferson could have fathered Sally Heming's children.
2. David Rice Atchison served as president of the United States for a day, although he is not counted in the numbering of presidents.
3. We now know that Abraham Lincoln was gay.

IRAQ WAR

1. The Iraq War has lasted longer than the Vietnam War, cost more and resulted in more Americans killed.
2. Sen. Hillary Clinton, D.Y., opposed the war in Iraq from the beginning of it.
3. The BBC reported before the war that President Vladimir Putin of Russia had warned President George W. Bush that the Russian secret service had learned Saddam Hussein was planning terrorist attacks on the United States.

INVENTORS

1. Congress has recognized Antonio Meucci, not Alexander Graham Bell, as the inventor of the telephone.
2. Television was invented by a 14-year-old farmboy named Philo T. Farnsworth while he was plowing a field.
3. Al Gore did not invent the Internet, but it could be argued that a Bush – Vanever Bush – did.

ENVIRONMENT AND ENERGY

1. When a woman in Maine accidentally broke a new energy-saving compact fluorescent light bulb, the state Environmental Protection Department called in a hazardous-waste-disposal team to clean up the mercury in it and billed her $2,000.
2. The United States has not built any oil refineries in more than 30 years.
3. The taxes on a gallon of gasoline are more than average oil company profits on the gallon.

QUOTATIONS

1. President John F. Kennedy's famous statement at the Berlin wall "Ich bin ein Berliner" actually means "I am a jelly doughnut."
2. The quote "With great power comes great responsibility" actually originated in a Spider-Man comic book.
3. Willie Sutton said, "I rob banks because that's where the money is."

FAMOUS PEOPLE
1. Lady Godiva's naked horseback ride was to persuade her husband to lower taxes on the peasants.
2. Ben Franklin discovered electricity.
3. Adolf Hitler's real last name was Shicklgruber.

THE ECONOMY
1. Most economists say minimum wage increases hurt the poor, especially minorities.
2. American women earn only 59 cents for every dollar men make.
3. America has lost more jobs than it has created as a result of NAFTA, and the new jobs tend to pay less.

STATISTICS
1. There are more federally licensed gun dealers than McDonald's restaurants in the United States.
2. The top 5 percent of wage earners pay less in taxes than those at the bottom.

EXERCISE: NUMBERS

PERCENTAGES
1. The City Council allotted $10,000 to the Springfield Arts Commission this year, $8,000 last year.
a. What was the percent of the increase?

b. What percentage less was last year's budget compared to this year's?

c. Last year's budget was what percent of this year's?

d. This year's budget is what percent of last year's?

2. Are the following percentages correct? If not, what should they be?
a. The cost for renting the hall went up 150 percent, from $150 last year to $225 this year.

b. After completion of last year's special bridge-repair campaign, the county's Road and Bridge Department spending will drop sharply this year, from a budgeted $3 million last year to only $1 million this year, a cut of 300 percent.

AVERAGES VS. MEDIANS
3. These were the scores on a test in a graduate-student seminar: 100, 98, 95, 93, 93, 90, 88, 87, 87, 86, 85, 85, 84, 71.
a. What was the average score?

b. What was the median?

PER CAPITA RATES
4. If a state budgets $100 million for a program that benefits half a million people, what is the per capita expenditure?

INTEREST RATES
5. If you take out a 10-year loan for $10,000 at 14 percent compounded annually, what is the total amount you will pay?

INFLATION
6. The CPI in January 1952 was 26.5 and 211.08 in January 2008. If a car cost $2,400 in January 1952, what would that equal in January 2008 dollars?

SALES TAXES

7. What would the sales tax be on a purchase of $32.50 if the state charges an 8 percent sales tax?

PROPERTY TAXES

8. The millage rate in 2007 for Plymouth, Mich., was 39.7366. If your home was assessed at $220,000, what would your property tax be?

EXERCISE: OBJECTIVITY

A. List the four rules typically referred to by the term "journalistic objectivity."

1.

2.

3.

4.

B. What's nonobjective about these statements?

5. The controversial, arch-conservative speaker of the House has definitely stirred up a hornet's nest with his latest dramatic proposal for additional widespread cuts.

6. Food is so bad at the Jackson prison that inmates have begun a hunger strike.

7. Black presidential hopeful Sen. Barack Obama, D-Ill., today criticized President Bush's handling of the war with Iraq.

8. The suspect was described as an Arab man of average height and build.

9. The grandmother of five claimed that if elected she would bring to the office a greater sense of caring for the disadvantaged than her predecessor.

10. The senator's humor is known to be as dry as a Kansas summer, when cows have been known to give powdered milk.

11. The U.S. Senate blocked funding Thursday for a Pentagon computer project that would violate the privacy rights of average Americans by scouring databases for terrorist threats.

C. Put the letter of the best answer in front of the number.

____12. Which of the following best summarizes a couple of the ways that editors introduce errors into stories?
a. trusting the reporter and not looking things up
b. writing headlines, captions and blurbs and rewriting the story
c. spicing up the story and not caring whether it's true
d. injecting their own racist or political views

_____13. Which one of the following attribution words would be most neutral?
a. answered
b. admitted
c. claimed
c. refuted

D. Circle O if the statement is written as objective journalism, N if it isn't.

O N   11 The bureaucrat in the registrar's office felt he would have to pay the disputed charge.

O N   12. He doubts the fact it happened as the Times had reported.

O N   13. Sampson believes the matter has been blown out of proportion.

EXERCISE: OBJECTIVITY IN A STORY FROM A PRESS RELEASE
Rewrite this press release into a proper news story by removing nonobjective language and putting it in AP style.

FISH

Everyone loves a fish fry.

So why not come out to the Springfield Baptist Church at 111 Elmwood Dr. this Saturday afternoon from 12:00 noon-3 o'clock in the afternoon? The public is invited to attend the festivities.

Meals will require a free-will donation of five dollars for each adult or three dollars per child for all you can eat. While you're chowing down, you can also enjoy the swinging sounds of the Accordionaires, as well as the Four Neat Guys, a Barbershop Quartet, that will entertain you with good clean wholesome music.

So mark your calendar, come on out, and bring your family. Proceeds will go to the Church building fund to help pay for the roof repairs after last month's storm. Remember, God loves you, and so do we!!!

EXERCISE: STORY EDITING
Edit the following story as directed by your instructor.

UNITED

The Springfield United Way today awarded $27,312 in supplemental appropriations to three agencies whose programs were threatened by inadequate funding.

The United Way Board of Directors gave $15,137 to the Rape Crisis Center to enable the center to operate through the end of the current physical year. Director Karen Gunter said the supplemental funds will help pay her salary and those of two part-time professional councilors.

The United Way board also awarded $10,000 to the Front Door, a personal crisis counseling center which caters to those with drug abuse and alcohol probelems. The agency will use the funds to pay higher rent at its new facility, 211 Hitt St. The old facility was condemned by the city.

A supplemental appropriation of $3,175 will go to the Boy Scouts for a sumeer camp program for disadvantaged youths. The amount matches a similar sum given to the Girl Scouts during the regular funding process last month.

During the regular funding process, the board had appropriated $1.37 million for 68 agencies in the county.

EXERCISE: STORY EDITING
Edit the following story as directed by your instructor.

TRAP

AUXVASSE — A 30-year-old Springfield man was trapped for nearly five hours Thursday when a bin collapsed, creating an avalanche of several tons of rock.

Roger Pickering was conscious when he finally was extricated by fire fighters and ambulance workers from Springfield and Callaway counties. He was taken by helicopter to University Hospital, where he was listed in serious condition, said John Metz of the Springfield County Volunteer Fire Department.

The rescuers had to be careful about shifting any of the rocks, because the wrong move could have crushed Pickering.

"It was a very bad situation, but thanks to the Springfield County Fire Department, things really worked smoothly," said Tony Townley, director of the Calloway County Ambulance District.

Pickering was cleaning the inside of a 60-foot-tall rock-handling machine at Auxvass Stone and Gravel at about 8:40 a.m. when the bin collapsed and buried him in rocks bigger than softballs, Townley said.

The machine is a funnel shaped bin that controls the flow of rocks and empties them onto a conveyor belt.

EXERCISE: STORY EDITING
Edit the following story as directed by your instructor.

RESCUE

A 5-month-old girl was rescued by Springfield police and firefighters during an early-morning blaze that destroyed a home in north-central Springfield on Saturday.

The fire, apparently caused by careless smoking, occurred one day before firefighters nationwide honor Fire Awareness Week, which officially starts today.

"The entire front end of the house was engulfed," said Division Chief George Glenn of the city Fire Department. "Flames where literally rolling out of the house."

Four children and three adults were sleeping in the home of John L. Williams at 805 Wilkes Blvd. about 12:20 a.m. when the fire started.

Springfield police officer Doug Parsons, the first to arrive on the scene, tried to rescue the infant, Treviona Bradford, who was sleeping in the rear bedroom. Parsons injured his foot while breaking a window to the home. Heavy smoke made entry impossible.

Firefighters who responded to the scene were able to vent smoke from the structure and gain entry, rescuing the child.

The infant was taken to University Hospital, where she was listed in critical condition in the burn unit Saturday.

EXERCISE: STORY EDITING
Edit the following story as directed by your instructor.

COUNCIL

Several bow-and-arrow enthusiasts came to Monday's Springfield City Council meeting to protest a regulation against arrow shooting within 50 yards of a residence, public park, trail or road.

"We have a problem with the regulation," said Dennis Ballard of the Springfield Area Archers. "It would essentially prohibit bow shooting in the city limits."

Fifth Ward Councilman Karl Kruse requested the report suggesting the 50-yard rule. The city staff decided against a total prohibition on arrow shooting because the State Department of Conservation has recorded only eight bow-hunting accidents in the last 10 years.

"The issue of bow hunting in the city is not really a public safety issue," Ballard said.

Kruse asked Ballard to submit his comments in writing. Kruse said he wanted to discuss the possible regulation with interested parties before the Council took any further action.

William Elder of 2105 Rock Quarry Road told Council members that bow hunting helps solve the city's deer-population problem. He said cars have killed many deer in his neighborhood.

"The only real solution is to kill them," Ballard said. "Anything we can do to encourage bow hunters is a wise move."

Later, Ballard said requiring bow hunters to take safety-training courses could relieve public concern about bow hunting.

In other business, the council:

•Decided to continue consideration of amendments to ordinances governing new mobile-home parks. With the changes, new parks could not contain homes built before 1976 and would have to provide sidewalks on both sides of all streets. Fourth Ward Councilman Rex Campbell requested considering minimum lot-size requirements.

•Appropriated funds for Williams Pipe Line Co. for their work with the Southampton Drive Reconstruction Project. The council had discussed not paying the bill because it twice exceeded the company's original estimate. City Manager Ray Beck said he would attempt negotiating a reduction in the bill's amount.

•Set a public hearing for the city's Paratransit Plan for Feb. 6. The plan is a guideline for public transportation for the disabled.

•Introduced an ordinance authorizing the city manager to enter an agreement with the United States Justice Department to obtain funds to pay 50 percent of the salaries for four police officers. The funds will come from the Federal Crime Bill and will pay a portion of the officers' salaries for a period of three years.

Student Name _____ Course _____ Date_____

EXERCISE: MACRO EDITING FOR THE BIG PICTURE

1. Analyze a lengthy story from your local newspaper. In the process, list any deficiencies in macro editing and describe what you would have done to fix the problem.

2. List some of the resources available to copy editors as they attempt to make certain that stories are accurate.

5

Macro Editing for Legality, Ethics and Propriety

Student Name _____ Course _____ Date_____

QUIZ: MEDIA LAW
Circle T for true, F for false.

T F   1. Although the First Amendment says there should be no laws abridging freedom of the press, the Constitution itself provides for copyright laws.

T F   2. Canada and Great Britain have more press freedom than the United States.

T F   3. No "prior restraint" means the government can't tell you what you can't publish, but it would not include telling you what you must publish.

T F   4. In America, the government can't use "prior restraint' on the press, but that doesn't mean a journalist couldn't be punished after the fact by a private lawsuit.

T F   5. Both print and broadcast media are licensed today in the United States.

T F   6. Freedom of the press means freedom to exercise editorial judgment.

T F   7. Freedom of the press is only an entitlement the government grants journalists as long as they act responsibly.

T F   8. "Freedom of the press" and the public's "right to know" mean the same thing.

T F   9. The right to know and the right to privacy are not explicitly mentioned in the Bill of Rights.

T F   10. The Supreme Court has said schools may censor school newspapers.

T F   11. Publishing obscene material is one of the few violations of media law that could land you in prison.

T F   12. "Libel" means you're held responsible.

T F   13. Any false story is libelous, especially if it hurts someone's feelings.

T F   14. The best way to avoid a libel problem is just with the word "alleged."

T F   15. Public officials and public figures have a harder time winning a libel suit than do average people.

T F   16. Don't worry about printing a slanderous statement by someone else because you're not saying it, you're just quoting it, so that will protect you from a libel suit.

T F   17. When covering either an accident or crime story, be careful not to convict someone in print or on the air who hasn't been convicted in court.

T F   18. The "a man" technique is the attribution of a quote to an anonymous source.

T F   19. Rather than saying that Bill Jones was driving drunk, veered into the oncoming lane and hit the victim's car head-on, it's better just to report that Jones "received a ticket" for doing that.

T F   20. It's not illegal to print a confession, but many papers avoid them until admitted in court because confessions are sometimes thrown out.

T F   21. It's a bad idea to assume that because the details in the story are right that a libelous headline or caption won't be actionable.

T F   22. If a journalist can prove a libelous statement is true, she should win a libel suit.

T F   23. A police officer's statement that someone is guilty would be legally protected if said in court but not necessarily if said elsewhere.

T F 24. If you make a factual mistake in a review that ends up damaging a restaurant's business, you would be protected by the "fair comment and criticism" provision.

T F 25. Publishing a joke that sullies the reputation of a dead person may not be ethical, but it would be legally protected.

T F 26. Public officials and public figures face a harder time winning a libel case than do ordinary people.

T F 27. If a story fairly presents both sides of a controversy about someone's reputation, that would be protected from a libel suit in all 50 states.

T F 28. Printing a correction admits fault for libel but may prevent a lawsuit or provide some legal protection in case one is filed.

T F 29. Printing the name and address of a witness to a major crime while the suspect is loose could conceivably result in a negligence lawsuit.

T F 30. Predicting in a news story that someone will be charged could result in a lawsuit if the person isn't.

T F 31. A homicide is not a "murder" until someone is convicted of murder.

T F 32. A "robbery" cannot occur in a house if the victim wasn't there when a theft happened.

T F 33. The best defense against an invasion of privacy lawsuit is usually newsworthiness.

T F 34. Generally speaking, a picture taken at a public event does not require signed releases to avoid invading privacy.

T F 35. A shopping mall is considered public property and does not require permission before taking pictures for a story.

T F 36. Some states have laws against secret taping, which could technically make some investigative stories involving cameras or microphones illegal or violations of privacy.

T F 37. "False-light" invasion of privacy is one privacy charge in which truth is a defense.

T F 38. Even in states with shield laws, a judge may order a journalist to reveal the name of an anonymous source.

T F 39. The standard for what's obscene depends on the community.

T F 40. Printing a story about a raffle to raise money for a child's operation could cause your paper to lose its mailing permit unless the raffle sponsors have obtained a state license.

T F 41. Lowercasing a brand name like Jell-O to make it generic could result in a letter from the manufacturer threatening a lawsuit if you do it again.

T F 42. The Fairness Doctrine said broadcasters must supply "equal time" when requested.

T F 43. Broadcasters no longer have to make sure conflicting viewpoints are given opportunity on controversial issues, but they do still have to provide all candidates in a primary or general election equal opportunity to buy time at the lowest rate.

T F 44. News coverage is exempt from Section 315's provision for time for candidates.

T F 45. The FCC bans indecency at all hours.

T F 46. Broadcast station owners must show every seven years at license-renewal time that the station has operated in the public interest.

T F 47. It's safer to assume laws that apply to both print and broadcast also apply to the Internet.

T F 48. Attempts to regulate Internet content have largely failed in the courts.

T F 49. An Internet provider is more likely to face legal problems if it tries to moderate its content than if it doesn't.

QUIZ: AMERICAN LEGAL SYSTEM
Circle T for true, F for false.

T F   1. Police make the final decision as to whether charges will be filed against a suspect.

T F   2. Only a defendant in a criminal trial may file an appeal, not the prosecution, but either side – the plaintiff or defendant – may appeal in a civil suit.

T F   3. A "tort" is another term for a misdemeanor.

T F   4. In a criminal case, the judge may take the case away from the jury to order a dismissal but not to overturn a verdict. A judge in a civil trial, however, may overturn a jury's verdict but usually just decides the amount of damages to be awarded if any.

T F   5. Proof required in a criminal case is "preponderance of evidence" but "beyond a reasonable doubt" in a civil case.

T F   6. Media law is almost exclusively civil law in the United States today and is determined primarily by courts rather than legislatures.

T F   7. The common law is based primarily on statutes.

T F   8. Equity law is made by a judge rather than a jury.

T F   9. Injunctions and restraining orders are examples of equity law because they apply before someone has done something whereas common law applies only to relief after someone has done something.

T F   10. The law of libel and invasion of privacy is most often determined by common law and the law of equity.

T F   11. Obscenity is usually determined on the basis of common law.

T F   12. An executive order by the president is the highest law of the land.

T F   13. The highest media law in the land is the First Amendment to the Constitution in the Bill of Rights.

T F   14. State constitutions don't guarantee freedom of the press because it's already guaranteed in the federal one.

T F   15. There are 52 court systems in the United States – federal courts, state courts and courts for the District of Columbia.

T F   16. Members of supreme courts are called "judges" except for the "chief justice of the Supreme Court."

T F   17. The U.S. Supreme Court invented the idea that it could rule a law unconstitutional and that it could review state court decisions – those powers aren't in the Constitution.

T F   18. Congress could legally abolish all federal courts in the United States other than the Supreme Court and decide on a different number of Supreme Court justices if it wanted to – these matters aren't predetermined in the U.S. Constitution.

T F   19. U.S. Circuit Courts are appeals courts.

T F   20. U.S. District Courts are federal trial courts.

T F   21. A Court of Appeals decision on federal matters is binding on all federal and state courts in its region only although others may look to it as a precedent.

T F   22. A trial court is a fact-finding court whereas an appeals court is a law-reviewing court. Testimony is not taken in an appeals court.

T F 23. Media law cases are usually heard first in a state court.

T F 24. Federal judges are appointed by the president for life unless the judge is impeached. State judges are elected in about half the states, appointed in the others, but states typically require they stand for re-election.

Student Name _____ Course _____ Date_____

PROBLEMS: MEDIA LAW

1. In your opinion, is censorship ever justified? For example, would you approve of regulating children's television, radio talk shows, the Internet or advertising? Should racist or sexist speech, hate speech, obscenity or profanity be illegal? Should the government censor something that's not politically correct or socially irresponsible? Should the government censor ideas that aren't true?

2. What do you consider the strongest argument against censorship and why?

3. Do you think electronic media should be as unregulated as print media? Why or why not? Why should it matter to print journalists?

4. Does the First Amendment contradict the Constitution in that the First Amendment says Congress shall make no law abridging freedom of the press but the Constitution provides for copyright laws to be passed? Also, do laws against fraud and perjury contradict the provisions for freedom of speech and the press even though no one seems to object? Or is there some distinction that would philosophically permit copyright and fraud laws on some other grounds?

5. Is it always illegal to libel someone? If not, when is it acceptable?

6. What does an average person have to prove to win a libel suit against you? What does a public figure or public official have to prove?

7. If a reporter has heard rumors that the president of a local university is embezzling, would it be OK to scoop other news outlets by reporting it as a rumor even though the reporter doesn't yet have evidence?

8. Are journalists given special protection in breaking the law in a sting-type story, using hidden cameras or secret taping, or going on someone else's property without permission to get a story?

9. Would it be OK to use a file photo of someone in a short dress, lots of makeup and leaning against a lamp post to illustrate a story on prostitution?

10. Is there any problem quoting from published sources or lifting a photo or illustration from a published source as long as it's attributed?

EXERCISE: EDITING SENTENCES FOR LEGAL OR ETHICAL PROBLEMS
How would you edit the following sentences, or what questions would you ask?

1. John Pelousky, 110 Hitt St., allegedly raped the victim, Angela Cartolini, at her apartment at 1320 Shady Ave.

2. Police arrested Pelousky on suspicion of rape.

3. The prosecutor's office will file charges against Pelousky on Wednesday.

4. Sgt. William Barnes of the Springfield police said Pelousky was "guilty, without a doubt."

5. The district attorney told the jury Pelousky was "guilty, without a doubt."

6. The food at Joe's Diner was the worst I have ever tasted.

7. Police say his arrest solves as many as 13 recent burglaries in the area.

8. Timothy Weeks, 12, was arrested for possession of a handgun after he showed it to a friend on the school playground.

9. The alleged assailant, Jonathan Andrews, fled the scene when police arrived.

10. Charlene Agate, Snipes' 7-year-old victim, was taken to St. Joseph's Hospital, where doctors examined her after the rape.

11. The prosecuting attorney said Johnson confessed the marijuana was his but denied he had intended to sell it.

Student Name _____ Course _____ Date_____

QUIZ: MEDIA ETHICS, TASTE AND SENSITIVITY
Circle T for true or F for false.

T F 1. Although not legally required, it's a good idea either not to print the name of a suspect who's been arrested but not charged, or if you print the name to point out that no charges have been filed.

T F 2. It's illegal to print the name of a victim of a sex crime or the name of a juvenile victim or suspect.

T F 3. It's legally permissible to publish confessions or the names of rape victims or juvenile defendants, but papers may choose not to for ethical reasons.

T F 4. In dealing with ethical questions, it's helpful to find out whether your newspaper has a written ethics policy, although many do not.

T F 5. Wearing a campaign button or having a political bumper sticker on your car could be considered an ethics violation at many newspapers.

T F 6. Letting a source you cover pick up the tab for a meal at which you interview her could be considered accepting a freebie and thus an ethics violation.

T F 7. Stressing the most sensational angle for the sake of an interesting lead is generally considered wrong but is often done.

T F 8. Selecting material to fit a preconceived lead or sense of the story is commonly done but could be seen as an ethics violation.

T F 9. Taking sides, even unconsciously, in what purports to be an objective story could be a violation of ethics.

T F 10. Most newspapers would probably not allow reporters to accept money for speaking to a group or organization they cover.

T F 11. Newspaper policies uniformly condemn accepting a freebie of any kind, including books to review or free admission to sporting events.

T F 12. It's never ethical to print information that is embarrassing to someone, no matter how newsworthy.

T F 13. Most newspapers would probably find it ethically acceptable to run a story exposing how a common current con is run even though someone might learn from the story how to do it.

T F 14. If someone holding hostages had as a demand that news outlets print or broadcast a manifesto of his, journalists should strongly debate the matter before running it.

T F 15. Being shy and giving in too easily to sources requests can pose ethical problems.

T F 16. When considering ethical problems in journalism, it's a good idea to consider not only the local ethics policy but also the general policies throughout the profession on this matter as well as your own beliefs.

T F 17. Newspapers usually reject pictures with nudity, obscene gestures or gore.

T F 18. Photos of tragedy and grief are just good drama, not something to worry about publishing.

T F   19. Journalists should strive for sensitivity in language in order to be politically correct.

T F   20. If something was not prejudicial in intent, you don't need to worry that it might be prejudicial in effect.

T F   21. If a stereotype in a story is a positive one – such as implying all Asian Americans are at the top of the class academically – then it's not offensive.

T F   22. A story should not describe a woman's appearance if it wouldn't a man's in a similar situation.

T F   23. It's a good idea to include women and minorities in stories that have nothing to do with their being women or minorities.

T F   24. "Black" is now considered an offensive term.

T F   25. "Disabled" is usually preferable to "handicapped," although it's best to follow local preference.

Student Name _____ Course _____ Date_____

PROBLEMS: ETHICS SITUATIONS

1. Would you be willing to print a false story to help authorities trap a terrorist?

2. Would you be willing to print stolen documents or information obtained from misrepresentation?

3. Would you accept freebies from publicity agents, such as a trip to Cancun if you were a travel writer? How about free tickets, books, albums,, food, etc.?

4. Should you be able to express your political views, openly run for office, write speeches for candidates, sign petitions, wear buttons or put bumper stickers for candidates or causes on your car? What if you're not covering stories about such things?

5. When should a paper print the name of someone suspected in a crime – when the suspect has been arrested, charged or convicted? Of a juvenile offender? Of a victim of a sexual assault? When should a paper report a suspect has confessed?

6. Is the common practice of printing ages and addresses a violation of privacy?

7. If you found out information in advance about the day of a U.S. attack on an enemy, our troop strength or the military strategy, should you report it?

8. Should you cooperate with authorities by being willing to turn over unpublished notes, photographs, recordings, etc. and submit to debriefing from authorities after covering a demonstration or returning from assignment in the Middle East?

9. Your paper has a policy never to use certain words in the paper, including the word "nigger." While editing a story about a Martin Luther King Day rally, you discover that one of the most powerful quotes in it is from a man who says, "I'm marching because I want my son to grow up in a world where he never has to listen to someone call him 'nigger.'" Do you print the quote as is?

10. Your paper has an exclusive interview with a man condemned to be executed for murdering his girlfriend. He comes across in the interview as completely unrepentant and at one point says, "I'm glad I killed the bitch!" The copy editor who edits the story writes a headline with the man's name (he's well-known now), followed by a colon to show attribution, followed by the quote just given. If you're the slot person, do you approve the headline?

11. A public official who has been much criticized lately in the media holds a press conference. With cameras rolling, he pulls out a revolver, holds it to his head and squeezes the

trigger. Your photography department pitches at the editors' budget meeting (where decisions are made about Page One) a package for the front page of a series of photos, dramatically showing the gun coming to the head and ending with the side of the official's skull being blown off. As copy-desk chief, the person who will lay out the page, what is your reaction?

12. It's the first day of school, and the photography department gives you a feature photo to run on the front of the local section of a boy crying and trying to hold on to his mother at the school gate. The boy is not identified by name in the caption information, but it says he's in the sixth grade at Springfield Elementary. Any problem?

Student Name _____ Course _____ Date_____

QUIZ: MACRO EDITING

IS IT AN ETHICAL OR A LEGAL PROBLEM?
Circle E if printing the following is only an ethical issue or L if it's also a legal problem for journalists.

E L   1. The names of victims of sexual assault.

E L   2. The names of juvenile victims, juvenile suspects or juveniles with convictions.

E L   3. The names of suspects who have been arrested but not charged as of deadline.

E L   4. Confessions.

E L   5. A police officer telling a journalist that a suspect is guilty.

It's legally permitted to print this, but it's a legal issue, not merely ethical.

E L   6. A district attorney telling a jury that a suspect is guilty.

E L   7. Calling a suspect in a murder case an "alleged murderer" or a "suspected murderer."

E L   8. Swear words.

Ethical for print journalists; Legal for broadcasters, depending on the words used.

E L   9. A picture of the annual Naked Mile at the University of Michigan that clearly shows participants' private parts.

E L 10. Posing as a police officer to obtain information from someone.

EXERCISE: STORY EDITING
Edit the following story as directed by your instructor.

MILK

Mark Orange didn't cry over spilled milk when the truck he was driving was sideswiped at 6:30 AM. Wednesday morning and spilled about 500 gals. of milk.

"I'm just happy nobody was hurt," he said. "Cows can give more milk, but people can't be replaced."

Police said a 2004 Ford Focus driven by Celia Schneider, 23, 316 Penny Lane swerved, and struck the Briar Dairy delivery truck. Schneider said she had swerved to avoid hitting a boy on a bicycle who crossed the street in front of her car.

Schneider, heading south on 3rd Street, was on her way home from her night job at State Farm Insurance Co. when she struck the milk truck.

Orange, 1617 Bach St., said that when he unsuccessfully swerved to try to avoid the car, the truck turned on its side, spilling milk onto the street.

Orange said he had not seen a boy on a bicycle.

"I think she's lying about that to try to avoid responsibility for her own recklessness," he said.

When police arrived, they were unable to locate a bicyclist at the scene.

Police Officer Wendell Phipps gave Schneider a sobriety test but said there was no evidence of alcohol use.

No one was injured in the accident and no charges were filed.

Damages are estimated at $2,000 to the Focus and $4,500 to the milk truck, according to police. Damages to the dairy products were estimated at $3,000.

Student Name _____ Course _____ Date_____

EXERCISE: STORY EDITING
Edit the following story as directed by your instructor.

BUSY

Crime may not pay, but it may have kept a 17 year old Springfield black man busy.

Springfield police said Patrick Jones of 308 Oak St. confessed to 21 burglaries after his arrest early Tuesday morning for breaking into the Anderson Hayes Day Care Center, 403 Park Ave.

Jones did not give up easily. When five police officers responded to the 5:30 a.m. call, Jones lead them on a chase down Providence Road, said Sgt. Drew Wheeler.

He didn't run fast enough.

"He ran west onto the overpass and laid down to conceal himself from the officers", Wheeler said. "It didn't work" .

During a two hour questioning, Jones admitted to the other burglaries.

Two of the break ins occurred the same day that Jones was arrested at the day care center.

Restaurants were Jones's favorite target. He confessed to allegedly breaking into Mazzio's Pizza, 70 E. Broadway, four times in as many months.

Mark Petersen, Mazzio's manager, said the Jones broke one of the door windows and took quarters out of the game machines and juke box.

Jones apparently enjoyed working holidays. He confessed to burglarizing Chinese Delicacies, 47 E. Broadway, on Christmas Eve and again on New Year's Eve.

The owner of the restaurant said money from the cash register and eight bottles of vintage Chinese wine were taken.

"I told the police the value of the wine was about $300, but you can't get it anymore. It's priceless," David Chou said.

Wheeler said Jones allegedly took from $45 to $250 in cash or property at each burglary. The prosecutor's office filed charges against Jones for burglary. He is being held in the Springfield jail in lieu of $25,000 bail.

Student Name _____ Course _____ Date_____

EXERCISE: STORY EDITING
Edit the following story as directed by your instructor.

ARRESTS

A Springfield electrician was arrested Tuesday at his home for allegedly threatening a neighbor with a gun.

Albert Crow, 42, was arrested on suspicion of second-degree assault and a weapons violation after the victim reported the incident to the police, said Policeman Bill Wheeler of the Springfield Police Department.

Crow was paroled on $10,000 bond.

In a separate incident, a Springfield man was arrested on suspicion of assaulting a Springfield woman.

Bill Regude, 40, of 902 Jefferson St., was arrested when he threw a bottle of floor wax at a woman that struck the brunette in the head, Wheeler said.

He said the dispute began when the mother of two inquired about several hundred dollars she said Regude allegedly owed her. Regude was charged with second-degree assault. He was released on $5,000 bond.

EXERCISE: STORY EDITING
Edit the following story as directed by your instructor.

FIREWORKS

CHESAPEAKE, Ohio (AP) — A prosecutor says he won't charge three people suspected of daring a mentally disabled man to set a fire that killed eight people in a fireworks store.

Each suspect was interviewed several times and took polygraph tests that showed "absolutely no evidence of deception," J.B. Collier Jr. said Friday.

Todd Hall, 24, is charged with eight counts of involuntary manslaughter in the July 3 fire at the Ohio River Fireworks store in Scottown, 100 miles southeast of Columbus.

About 40 shoppers were in the store when Hall allegedly held a lighted cigarette to a box of firecrackers. Twelve people were injured in the fire.

In court for a preliminary hearing Friday, Hall blurted out, "I didn't mean to hurt anybody."

He touched two fingers to his forehead in a salute toward victims' families as he entered Lawrence County Municipal Court and stuck his tongue out at a reporter.

Hall's attorney, Richard Wolfson, had no comment about the prosecutor's decision not to charge anyone else in the case.

Authorities had said they believed others who were with Hall dared him to light the fireworks. Hall underwent a lobotomy because of injuries he suffered in a skateboard accident in 1987 in Morgantown, W.Va. The portion of his brain that was removed controls thinking, memory and judgment.

The names of the three were never released.

Judge Donald Capper bound the case over to a grand jury that will meet Aug. 5. Hall, of Proctorville, was returned to the county jail on $500,000 bond.

Collier also said the store's sprinkler system, which was believed to have malfunctioned, had been turned off and showed evidnce of tampering. He said authorities did not know who might have done the tampering.

AP-CS-07-13 0742EDT

EXERCISE: STORY EDITING
Edit the following story as directed by your instructor.

INFANT

MARTINEZ, Calif. (AP) — A 6-year-old boy charged with the near-fatal beating of an infant is not competent to stand trial, a judge has ruled.

Juvenile Referee Stephen K. Easton suspended criminal proceedings against the boy Friday, saying that juvenile courtrooms are "not designed for 6-year-old kids."

Easton ruled the boy couldn't help in his defense against charges of assault with great bodily harm and trespass in the April beating of 1-month-old Ignacio Bermudez Jr.

The case is now on schedule to be reviewed about every six months. The 6-year-old, who did not attend the hearing Friday, will remain at a group home, said his lawyer, John Burris.

Burris said he will ask that charges be dropped but wants to ensure the boy will receive treatment.

"He is a child that needs intensive therapeutic treatment, and I am prepared for that to continue as long as the doctor says he needs it — and that's indefinitely at this point," Burris said.

AP-CS-07-13 0536EDT

6

Micro Editing
for Precision in Language

Student Name _____ Course _____ Date_____

QUIZ: MICRO EDITING FOR PRECISION IN LANGUAGE
GRAMMAR AND USAGE
Circle T for true or F for false.

T F   1. Micro editing is important because if the details aren't mastered, they distract from what is – the information the writer is trying to convey.

T F   2. If something is written to look like a sentence but lacks a subject or verb or doesn't express a complete thought, it's a "fragment."

T F   3. "Fused sentences" and "comma-splice sentences" both involve two sentences jammed together improperly – the first without any punctuation between them, the second with only a comma between them.

T F   4. Every long sentence is a "run-on sentence."

T F   5. Reader stoppers and false connections are examples of ways that writing can confuse readers.

T F   6. W.C. Fields' famous line that, "Sometimes we must take the bull by the tail and face the situation" is an example of a "mixed metaphor."

T F   7. A pronoun must clearly refer to and agree with its antecedent.

T F   8. Nominative-case pronouns must be used for subjects of clauses and for pronouns that follow a linking verb.

T F   9. Objective-case pronouns must be used for all objects as well as the subject of an infinitive.

T F 10. The only kind of pronoun that can act like an adjective in front of a gerund is an objective-case pronoun.

T F 11. "That" or "which" -- not "who" or "whom" -- should be used when referring to any animal.

T F 12. "Which" should be used instead of "that" when introducing something parenthetical that should have a comma before it.

T F 13. To decide whether to use "who" or "whom," start reading the sentence after the choice between the two but adding "he" or "him" to complete the thought. If "he" works, use "whom," but if "him" works, use "who."

T F 14. The only time an apostrophe is used to make a nonpossessive word plural is when it's the plural of a numeral.

T F 15. To make a noun plural that already ends in *s,* add *'s.*

T F 16. Make a noun possessive by adding *'s* if it doesn't end in *s* or is not a name or a plural, and the next word doesn't start with *s.*

T F 17. All tenses of a verb in English can be formed if you know its "principal parts."

T F 18. "Passive voice" refers to when the subject of a clause is being acted upon rather than doing the acting. It should be used only when you want to stress the receiver of the action, not the doer.

83

T F 19. When something is not now true but *could, might* or *would* be under a certain condition, don't use *can, may* or *will.*

T F 20. If a verb expresses a condition contrary to fact, you should make sure its proper subjunctive-mood form is used.

T F 21. A conjunction in the subject influences the number of the verb, but a preposition between the subject and verb does not.

T F 22. Collective nouns *always* take singular verbs.

T F 23. Indefinite pronouns and certain uncountable nouns are singular even though they look plural or seem plural in meaning.

T F 24. Fractions and percentages are singular when referring to number of things but plural when referring to the amount of one thing.

T F 25. Use an adjective when describing a noun or pronoun, but use an adverb to describe a verb or other modifier.

T F 26. Modifiers should be placed whenever possible next to the word they describe.

T F 27. When two modifiers are in a row, you generally put a comma between them if you could reverse them and put *and* between them.

T F 28. When two modifiers in a row couldn't be reversed, you usually put a hyphen between them if the first modifies the second.

T F 29. Interjections take either an exclamation mark or a comma after them, depending on the amount of emotion.

T F 30. You should try to avoid ending a sentence with a preposition.

T F 31. Many newspapers won't let you split a prepositional phrase across lines of a headline, but you should if the preposition is really part of the verb.

T F 32. You should never start a sentence with *and* or *but.*

T F 33. Always put a comma between dependent and independent clauses.

T F 34. "Not only" takes "but also" because they are correlative conjunctions.

T F 35. Usage is mainly a matter of vocabulary – but of the proper use of small, everyday words, not so much big, unusual words.

Student Name _____ Course _____ Date_____

QUIZ: OVERVIEW OF STYLE, SPELLING AND TIGHTENING
Circle T for true, F for false.

T F   1. The main stylebook journalists use is that of *The New York Times.*

T F   2. "Style," as journalists use the term, refers to a writer's individual way with words.

T F   3. Days of the week are never abbreviated.

T F   4. Months are abbreviated only before a date, states only after a city.

T F   5. Months and states with short names are never abbreviated.

T F   6. The only names for thoroughfares that are abbreviated are "avenue," "boulevard" and "street," and only after a street address.

T F   7. Ampersands, cents marks and percentage marks are not normally used. Instead the words are written out.

T F   8. Common nouns are lowercase, and proper nouns are uppercase.

T F   9. In English, we capitalize the names of days and months.

T F 10. Capitalize the names of varieties of animals, food and plants.

T F 11. Department names are always capitalized, including the word "department."

T F 12. Regions are normally capitalized, but directions are not.

T F 13. Trade names should be capitalized or a generic term substituted when appropriate.

T F 14. AP lowercases pronouns referring to God or Jesus but capitalizes "Mass" and "Communion."

T F 15. One-digit numbers are usually written out but numbers above written with numerals.

T F 16. Numerals are always used, no matter the number of digits, for certain things like addresses, ages, measurements, money, percentages and years.

T F 17. The only numeral that can start a sentence is a year.

T F 18. "Million," "billion" and "trillion" are always written out.

T F 19. Independent clauses joined by a conjunction need a comma before the conjunction.

T F 20. Journalists don't usually put a comma before the word "and" in a series.

T F 21. If the sentence continues, journalists put a comma both before and after a year following a date or a state following a city.

T F 22. Journalists typically only use semicolons between items in a series when at least one of them contains a comma.

T F 23. Capitalize after a colon only if what follows is a complete sentence.

T F 24. Dashes may be used for dramatic pauses or in place of commas around parenthetical items containing commas.

T F 25. Every quote needs to be attributed, but every paraphrase does not.

T F 26. When shifting from one speaker to another in a story, it's better to put the attribution before the quote from a different person.

T F 27. The better order is usually source said, not said source.

T F 28. When used as attribution, "believes," "feels," "hopes" or "thinks" imply mind reading.

85

T F 29. When attribution comes before a paraphrase or quote, there should always be a comma after the "said."

T F 30. When attribution comes after a paraphrase or single-sentence quote, there should always be a comma before the attribution.

T F 31. The first word of a quotation should not be capitalized if it neither starts a full-sentence quote and is not a proper noun.

T F 32. Periods and commas always go inside the quote marks when they come at the end of a quotation, but exclamation marks and question marks depend on whether they were part of the quote.

T F 33. You should not go from a partial quote and a full-sentence one within the same paragraph.

T F 34. Always put a quotation mark at the end of a paragraph even if the quote continues in the next paragraph.

T F 35. Rather than use ellipses to show missing words, journalists typically use partial quotes or paraphrases.

T F 36. Newspapers tend to avoid parentheses.

T F 37. Journalists usually use the day to describe events within a week of publication forward or backward, a date for anything beyond that time.

T F 38. If a street name contains a direction, like "West Maple," the direction is abbreviated in a street address.

T F 39. Official titles are always abbreviated.

T F 40. "President" and "professor" are only abbreviated in front of someone's name.

T F 41. Journalists normally don't use courtesy titles like "Mr." or "Mrs."

T F 42. Cities in datelines appear in all capital letters, but the state or country does not – just the first letter is capitalized.

T F 43. Washington is written without the D.C. and New York without the City.

T F 44. The official spelling source for journalists is the spell checker in Microsoft Word.

T F 45. If you've followed the wire-service rule for checking whether a compound word is one word, two words or hyphenated and not found it, make it two words as a noun or verb, or hyphenate it as a compound adjective in front of a noun.

T F 46. When tightening copy, it's important to make sure that the revision says exactly the same thing but in fewer, more common words.

EXERCISE: NOUNS AND PRONOUNS
Circle the correct or preferred form of the pronoun.

1. Roberto and (me, I) are going to El Paso next week.

2. The mayor said he thought that you, (he, him) and (she, her) should work more.

3. The police officer thought the woman in the car to be (I, me).

4. (She, Her) who wins the spelling contest will receive the certificate.

5. The suspect said that it was not (she, her) who committed the crime.

6. Did the crowd enjoy (him, his) playing the guitar?

7. Interview (whoever, whomever) comes to the door.

8. Ask (whoever, whomever) you will, the answer is still the same, the secretary said.

9. I talked to the winners of the race, (he, him) and (she, her).

10. It certainly was not (he, him) or (I, me) who stole it, the suspect said.

11. Award the certificate to (whoever, whomever) the speaker believes to be deserving.

12. Antoine Bylinsky is 100; can you imagine (his, him) jogging?

13. The dean asked the chairman and (I, me) to come to his office.

13. He thought the young woman in the last row to be (I, me).

15. Doesn't the comptroller recall (him, his) asking the mayor to do this?

16. No one recalls (who, whom) she said should compete first.

17. (Who, Whom) did the president say called him Monday night?

18. They have no objections to (you, your) going with them.

19. Both Latisha Jones and (she, her) enjoyed the (instructor, instructor's) laughing at the remark.

20. Award the trophy to (whoever, whomever) finishes first in the relay.

21. Award the prize to (whoever, whomever) she says should receive it.

22. The managing editor is making (we, us) writers a set of instructions.

23. (We, Us) early arrivals will have first choice of assignments.

24. "Can you imagine (me, my) doing such a foolish thing?" the president said.

25. Neither (he, him) nor his brothers are as short as (I, me).

26. The reporters were asked to meet (he, him) and (she, her) at the airport.

27. Was it (she, her) and (he, him) who met the star player?

28. No one enjoyed (his, him) talking on that subject.

29. It is not (I, me) who am needed; it is (she, her).

30. Give the award to (she, her), the president said.

Student Name _____ Course _____ Date_____

EXERCISE: VERBS
Circle the correct or preferred form within the parentheses.

1. The reporter spent her day off just (lying, laying) about the apartment.

2. Former President Bush (lay, laid) the book on the desk.

3. The secretary of the treasury said she had (laid, lain) the report on the table.

4. Aires (lay, laid) down on the couch.

5. The editor saw your stylebook (lying, laying) on the desk.

6. The exhausted woman had just (lain, laid) down when the baby cried.

7. The doctor said she was (lying, laying) on the beach when the attack occurred.

8. The writer (laid, lay) the story aside and answered the telephone.

9. That old dog likes to (lie, lay) in the shade.

10. The hospitalized woman said she shouldn't have (laid, lain) in the sun so long.

11. The oil (lays, lies) near the surface, geologists said.

12. The slain youngster's clothes were (lying, laying) about the house.

13. The nurse has been (sitting, setting) with the terminally ill patient since Sunday.

14. Police said the suspect just (set, sat) still and let them arrest him.

15. The candidate decided to (set, sit) quietly and await the results of the vote.

16. Two children (setting, sitting) in the back seat of the car were not hurt.

17. The boy was told not to (sit, set) on the table, and that may have saved his life.

18. The ushers (set, sat) extra chairs in the aisles to accommodate the huge crowd.

19. The utility company had (sat, set) the poles in concrete only a day before.

20. Fifty students (set, sat) waiting for the test to begin.

21. The children are (sitting, setting) in the trees.

22. The printers are (sitting, setting) type for the special section today.

23. As a hospital volunteer, he often (sets, sits) up late with a patient.

24. If you (sit, set) on that chair, you may fall on the floor, the senator said.

25. The Colorado River has been (rising, raising) all week as the dam's gates open.

26. The effect of the OPEC vote was to (rise, raise) oil prices again.

27. The players' hopes (raised, rose) and fell during the last quarter.

28. If gasoline prices (raise, rise) any higher, some will have to quit using their cars, he said.

29. The sun (raises, rises) at about 6 o'clock this time of year, the farmer said.

30. The cost of living is (raising, rising) rapidly in U.S. cities, the report shows.

31. The crew (raised, rose) the stage 3 feet for tonight's performance.

32. The caller said he saw smoke (raising, rising) from the old building.

33. With its extra passenger, the helicopter would not (rise, raise) quickly.

34. According to market reports, stocks have been (raising, rising) rapidly.

35. The mayor expected his decision to quit as chairman of the committee and (accepted, excepted) his letter of resignation.

36. Did the reporter (lose, loose) all his keys?

37. Please (lend, loan) the teacher your grammar book.

38. The noise from the construction project (aggravates, annoys, irritates) the students.

39. Some find that certain foods (aggravate, annoy, irritate) the skin.

40. The striking workers were told not to (aggravate, annoy, irritate) an already-tense situation.

Student Name _____ Course _____ Date_____

EXERCISE: ADJECTIVES AND ADVERBS
Circle the correct or preferred form within the parentheses.

1. Neither the mayor nor (he, him) (seem, seems) (happy, happily).

2. The landlord looked (angry, angrily) at Smith and (I, me).

3. The player looks (bad, badly) because of his injury.

4. Each woman (look, looks) (beautiful, beautifully) wearing (her, their) new outfit.

5. This drink tastes (sour, sourly) to (she, her) and (I, me).

6. From where we were working, the train's whistle sounded (loud, loudly).

7. The flowers (smell, smells) (sweet, sweetly) to (he, him).

8. The cook was told to cook the meat (tender, tenderly) so that it would taste (good, well).

9. The carpentry teacher told (we, us) students to make a piece of furniture (strong, strongly).

10. (His, Him) taking another job (make, makes) (we, us) journalists feel (sad, sadly).

11. Boil the eggs (hard, hardly) while (he, him) sets the table.

12. Natasha looked (happy, happily) because I believed (she, her).

13. The engine runs (smooth, smoothly) because (she, her) and (I, me) repaired it.

14. While Antonio and (I, me) (was, were) camping, the thunder sounded (loud, loudly).

15. The editor looked (proud, proudly) as the panel honored both (she, her) and (he, him).

16. Each of the graduate students (is, are) (happy, happily) about passing (his, their) comprehensive examinations.

17. The soldier (seem, seems) (happy, happily) to return to the United States.

18. She (doesn't have but, has but) one television set.

19. (This, These) kind of apples is worth the price.

20. Bill is the (older, oldest) of the two students.

21. The teacher chose a (real, really) fine day for the trip.

22. The disc jockey has (a lot of, many) albums.

23. To publish a (more perfect, perfect) magazine, the staff members must work together.

24. Does he feel (sure, surely) the reporter will keep his word?

25. (Sure, Surely) he feels that the reporter will keep his word.

26. The injured player feels (some, somewhat) better now.

27. The editor (cannot help but laugh, cannot help laughing) when she recalls what he said.

28. The news department (only has, has only) one computer terminal in operation.

29. See whether the reporter has (most, almost) completed the story.

30. The sportswriter said she has (quite a few, a number of) sources.

31. The copy editor edited the story (other, otherwise) than she was instructed.

32. Make the pizza crust (crisp, crisply).

33. The workers complained of feeling (poor, poorly).

34. The band played (poor, poorly) during halftime, the director said.

35. The children went to bed, but they (never, did not) (sleep, slept).

36. The new reporter is younger than (anyone, anyone else) on the staff.

37. The president looked (happy, happily) at his family as he took the oath of office.

38. The coach watched (proud, proudly) as her team received the trophy.

39. She (seldom ever, rarely) uses her bicycle.

40. The chief spoke (harsh, harshly) to the delinquent officers.

41. While camping, the group's supplies ran (low, lowly).

42. He is the most able of (any other, all) reporters on the newspaper staff.

43. The collector has stamps from (most, almost) all nations.

44. The managing editor seemed (rather, sort of) disgusted with the photography staff.

45. (Sure, Surely) the photographer was pleased to receive the honor.

46. The football players slept (sound, soundly) after the 10-hour trip.

47. Prepare the steaks (rare, rarely) for Paula and (he, him).

48. Usually, the committee meetings are (real, really) dull.

EXERCISE: PREPOSITIONS
Provide the correct preposition in each sentence. More than one may be a correct choice.

1. The sailors were told to go _____ the ship.

2. The reporter was initiated _____ the professional society.

3. The kangaroo is a species found only _____ Australia.

4. The soldiers had to contend _____ the problem of low morale.

5. The newspaper's survey compared the features of foreign automobiles _____ the features of American automobiles.

6. The new police reporter was frightened _____ the idea of writing about organized crime.

7. Each player must adhere _____ the rules.

8. The finder of the lost billfold was rewarded _____ cash.

9. They can subscribe _____ more than one daily newspaper.

10. The reporter lives _____ Providence Road _____ Springfield.

11. The patient died _____ pneumonia.

12. The waiter was told to wait _____ three tables.

13. Frances Altobelli now lives _____ an apartment.

14. The car collided _____ the truck.

15. She wrote the story in accordance _____ the editor's instructions.

16. The editor spoke for 30 minutes _____ the new copy editor.

17. Every student should listen attentively _____ the professor.

18. The streets run parallel _____ the city park.

19. The reporter was told not to meddle _____ matters of the city department.

20. Two committee members abstained _____ voting on the proposal.

21. Antonio Valdez prefers living on campus _____ living off campus.

22. Each reporter should concentrate _____ his or her work.

23. The story is almost free _____ style errors.

24. Friends confide _____ each other.

25. The writer was reluctant to part _____ the old typewriter.

26. Some people are not allergic _____ poison ivy.

27. Seniors dislike parting _____ classmates.

28. The reporter's work compares favorably _____ the work of another writer.

29. The managing editor told the reporter to try _____ complete the story before deadline.

30. The feature writer was disappointed _____ not getting the story.

31. The elderly man was accompanied _____ a hospital volunteer.

32. The officer's car was parked parallel _____ the other cars.

33. The news editor looked _____ while the repairman fixed the machine.

34. The commentator is careless _____ his appearance.

35. The news operation is independent _____ the advertising department.

36. According _____ the fire chief, the blaze could have been prevented.

37. In that sentence, the pronoun he is the antecedent _____ John Brown.

38. The car is parked _____ the house near the back door.

39. The train's passengers were deaf _____ the elderly woman's pleas for medical help.

40. The editor asked the reporter, "What do you infer _____ the mayor's comments?"

41 . The copy editor was told to substitute the second lead _____ the first lead.

42. The reporter is capable _____ writing the story.

43. The Police Department will keep the protesters _____ marching.

44. The jury did not agree _____ a verdict.

45. Mayor Harkin said her aide is one _____ whom she can confide.

EXERCISE: SUBJECT-VERB AGREEMENT
Circle the correct form within the parentheses.

1. Shelly Anderson, as well as Jones and (we, us), (was, were) late today.

2. Neither the chairman nor (she, her) (was, were) able to go to Washington.

3. (Has, Have) either Carter or (she, her) studied Latin?

4. Here (come, comes) the mayor and (they, them).

5. The editor and (I, me) thought it to be the coach and (she, her).

6. (Was, Were) you and (she, her) in the restaurant when the reporter and (he, him) called?

7. Every one of the players (was, were) at the airport to meet Shu-Mei and (I, me).

8. There (is, are) Hamilton and Rodriguez, as well as (she, her), talking with the dean and (he, him).

9. (Has, Have) her sister and (he, him) decided to go with you, (she, her) and (they, them)?

10. The chairman, as well as the professors, (is, are) kind to Steve and (I, me).

11. Laszlo, Bob and (I, me) (is, are) the committee.

12. A number of the members (has, have) visited Tai-en and (I, me).

13. Neither the chairman nor the professors (advise, advises) you and (I, me) to study Spanish next semester.

14. You, not (he, him), (is, are) the one (who, whom) the editor called.

15. Neither Pierre Aumente nor his son (was, were) able to assist (we, us) writers.

16. Susan, together with the rest of (we, us) juniors, (was, were) in Burbank last weekend.

17. Every girl and boy (is, are) responsible to the teacher.

18. The jury (has, have) agreed upon a verdict.

19. The media (is, are) invited to the meeting.

20. Biscuits and gravy (is, are) on the menu.

95

21. Five percent of the workers (is, are) absent.

22. The number of persons present (is, are) large.

23. Five miles (is, are) a long distance for someone (who, whom) cannot jog far.

24. The team (is, are) unable to reach a decision.

25. He is one of those persons (who, whom) (is, are) always late for class.

26. Many a one (has, have) been disappointed by another in (who, whom) he placed trust.

27. "Seven Beauties" (is, are) usually enjoyed by all (who, whom) understand Italian.

28. Magazines or books (is, are) an appropriate gift for (we, us) students.

29. Three fourths of the videotape (has, have) been saved.

30. You and (she, her) (is, are) accountable to someone in authority.

31. Do you think $150 (is, are) too much for each of these speakers?

32. Here (come, comes) the reporters (who, whom) you wish to hire.

33. The team (is, are) going to Brownsville.

34. Steak and eggs (is, are) one of his favorite dishes, Aurelio said.

35. This is one of those magazines that (is, are) popular with journalists (who, whom) you believe (is, are) well-informed.

36. That she writes no better than (we, us) (is, are) an accepted truth.

37. Each graduate and undergraduate (is, are) insistent upon talking to an adviser (who, whom) the chairman believes can answer important questions.

38. That you were thought to be (he, him) (is, are) hard to prove.

39. Where (is, are) those students (who, whom) you called?

40. Today's news (is, are) important to the advertising department.

41. Not only (she, her) but also (he, him) (think, thinks) that you should be the winner.

42. The committee (has, have) gone to Philadelphia.

43. Ham and cheese (is, are) his favorite sandwich.

44. Neither the reporter nor the editors (has, have) studied metaphysics.

45. He, not his brothers, (is, are) attending classes at the University of Rhode Island.

EXERCISE: PRONOUN-ANTECEDENT AGREEMENT
Circle the correct or preferred form within the parentheses.

1. Every reporter (was, were) asked to give (his or her, their) assistance.

2. Jacobs, as well as (we, us), (has, have) given (his or her, their) share.

3. Every one of you (is, are) responsible for (his or her, your, their) own copy.

4. Each writer must do (his or her, their) share.

5. No one wants to lose (his or her, their) books.

6. Not one of the clerks (has, have) had to decrease (his or her, their) work.

7. The students (has, have) lost (his or her, their) books.

8. Neither Rolando nor Ms. Barbieri could find (his, her, their) books.

9. The police chief, as well as the officers, (was, were) willing to do (her, their) work.

10. No woman or man should praise (himself, themselves) too highly.

11. Everybody who seeks the job must send (his or her, their) resume.

12. The panel (is, are) divided in (its, their) decision.

13. Not one of the reporters (think, thinks) that (she, her) can complete the story.

14. Every newspaper and magazine (has, have) (its, their) influence.

15. Each of the writers (has, have) put forth (his or her, their) best.

16. All persons should take care of (his or her, their) business.

17. Each person should take care of (his or her, their) business.

18. Either Brown or Smith will lend you (his or her, their) notes.

19. If anyone asks for me, tell (him or her, them) to call tomorrow.

20. Not one of the club members (is, are) doing (his or her, their) part.

21. No social worker cares to see (his or her, their) clients mistreated.

22. The man, as well as his brothers, (was, were) prepared to do (his or her, their) assignment.

23. Either Armando or Ms. Killian will offer you (his, her, their) advice.

24. Each of the scouts (has, have) completed (his or her, their) requirements.

25. The committee (is, are) not divided in (its, their) recommendation.

26. If Congress has (its, their) way, gun controls will be toughened.

27. The Police Department has (its, their) annual benefit concert this week.

28. The U.S. soccer team tied A.C. Milan in (its, their) first match of the season.

29. Jeff Francoeur's fan club packed the auditorium for a glimpse of (its, their) hero.

30. Each of the partygoers (was, were) asked to bring (his or her, their) favorite wine.

Student Name _____ Course _____ Date_____

EXERCISE: THE PARTS OF SPEECH

PREPOSITIONS
Provide the correct preposition in each sentence.

1. The reporter was initiated _____ the professional society.

2. The kangaroo is peculiar _____ Australia.

3. The soldiers had to contend _____ the problem of low morale.

4. The reporter was frightened _____ the idea of writing about organized crime.

5. The finder of the lost billfold was rewarded _____ cash.

6. The man died _____ cancer.

7. She wrote the story in accordance _____ the editor's instructions.

8. Two committee members abstained _____ voting on the proposal.

9. The managing editor told the reporter to try _____ complete the story before deadline.

10. The elderly man was accompanied _____ a hospital volunteer.

NOUNS AND PRONOUNS
Circle the correct or preferred form within the parentheses.

1. Joe, Paul and (me, I) are going to Detroit next week

2. I thought that you, (he, him) and (she, her) would work more.

3. The woman in the car was thought to be (I, me).

4. (She, Her) who wins the contest will receive the certificate.

5. Did you enjoy (him, his) playing the guitar?

6. Give the report to (whoever, whomever) comes to the door.

7. No one recalls (who, whom) she said should work first.

8. They have no objections to (you, your) going with them.

9. Yes, it was (they, them) about (who, whom) I was speaking.

10. It was (we, us) staff writers (who, whom) you saw.

SUBJECT-VERB AGREEMENT
Circle the correct or preferred form within the parentheses.

1. Ashley, as well as Miller and (we, us), (was, were) late today.

2. Neither the chairman nor (she, her) (was, were) able to go to Washington.

3. (Has, Have) either Carter or (she, her) studied Latin?

4. Here (come, comes) the mayor and (they, them).

5. There (is, are) Jiminez and Fitzgerald, as well as (she, her), talking with the dean.

6. (Has, Have) her sister and (he, him) decided to go with you, (she, her) and (they, them)?

7. Ronaldo, Antonio, and (I, me) (is, are) the committee.

8. Neither the chairman nor the professors (advise, advises) you and (I, me) to study Spanish next semester.

9. Latisha, together with the rest of (we, us) juniors, (was, were) in Scranton last weekend.

10. The media (is, are) invited to the meeting.

PRONOUN-ANTECEDENT AGREEMENT
Circle the correct or preferred form within the parentheses.

1. Every reporter (was, were) asked to give (his or her, their) help for the section.

2. Gianna, as well as (we, us), (has, have) given (his or her, their) share.

3. Every one of you (is, are) responsible for (his or her, your, their) own copy.

4. Each writer must do (his or her, their) share.

5. No one wants to lose (his or her, their) books.

6. None of us (think, thinks) that (he or she, him) can complete the story.

7. Every newspaper and magazine (has, have) (its, their) influence.

8. If anyone asks for me, tell (him or her, them) to call tomorrow.

9. Each of the scouts (has, have) completed (his or her, their) requirements.

10. The committee (is, are) not divided in (its, their) recommendation.

ADJECTIVES AND ADVERBS
Circle the correct or preferred form within the parentheses.

1. Neither the mayor nor (he, him) (seem, seems) (happy, happily).

2. The landlord looked (angry, angrily) at Smith and (I, me).

3. The player looks (bad, badly) because of his injury.

4. This drink tastes (sour, sourly) to (she, her) and (I, me).

5. The cook was told to cook the meat (tender, tenderly) so it would taste (good, well).

6. The soldier (seem, seems) (happy, happily) to return to the United States.

7. She (doesn't have but, has but) one television set.

8. (This, These) kind of apples is worth the price.

9. Enrique is the (older, oldest) of the two students.

10. (Sure, Surely) he feels that the reporter will keep his word.

VERBS
Circle the correct or preferred form within the parentheses.

1. The reporter spent her day off just (laying, lying) about the apartment.

2. She (lay, laid) her book on the desk.

3. The woman had just (lain, laid) down when the baby cried.

4. The old dog likes to (lie, lay) in the shade.

5. The nurse has been (sitting, setting) with the patient.

6. The ushers (set, sat) extra chairs in the aisles.

7. The utility company (sat, set) the poles in concrete.

8. The Colorado River has been (rising, raising) all week.

9. The effect of the OPEC vote was to (rise, raise) oil prices again.

10. The players' hopes (raised, rose) and fell during the last quarter.

EXERCISE: THE PARTS OF SPEECH
Identify the parts of speech in the following passages by indicating the usage above each word.

Three local residents, who allegedly lured a truck driver with offers of sex for money, then stabbed him in the chest, were bound over for trial at a preliminary hearing Tuesday in Springfield County Associate Circuit Court.

Mitchell Briggs, 22, of 1205 Third St., Bobbi Sue Stanton, 23, and Rhoda F. Mathews, both of 1406 Lynnwood Drive, remained free on bond. They were arrested in connection with the stabbing of Minnesota truck driver Scott Allen.

All three are charged with first-degree assault. Briggs is also charged with armed criminal action.

Allen testified that the women approached him at Midway Truck Plaza and asked whether he wanted to "party." He said they told him, "If you want to have a good time, that can cost you 50 bucks."

Now list the verbs or verb phrases in the above passage and indicate the person, number, tense, voice and mood of each.

Verb or phrase	Person	Number	Tense	Voice	Mood

EXERCISE: THE PARTS OF SPEECH
Identify the parts of speech in the following passages by indicating the usage above each word.

As Sikeston High School's Aaron Gleason trudged to the 18th green at A.L.Gustin Golf Course on Monday, he grimaced and held his chest.

The defending Class 4A state champion is not only battling 126 other golfers this week, but he also has a case of strep throat, which is causing him chest pains. Gleason said he has been taking antibiotics for two days, hoping he could regain his strength.

"I feel terrible," Gleason said softly as he sank onto a wooden bench at the first hole after making the turn. "My chest is killing me."

With nine holes remaining, Gleason was 7 over par. But he shot par on the back side and finished at 77, 8 strokes behind the leader, St. Joseph Central's Rob Verbeck.

Now list the verbs or verb phrases in the above passage and indicate the person, number, tense, voice and mood of each.

Verb or phrase	Person	Number	Tense	Voice	Mood

Student Name _____ Course _____ Date_____

EXERCISE: ACTIVE-PASSIVE VOICE
Circle the verbs in the passive voice in the following stories.

After five months of frustration, Springfield County authorities on Friday took a 16-year-old boy into custody for first-degree murder in connection with the Dec. 18 beating and stabbing death of Tammie Fortsam.

Sheriff's Department spokesman Michael Stubben said in a prepared statement that a pair of shoes was the crucial clue in the case. He would not comment on how investigators got the shoes, but his news release said "lab analysis" proved "the shoes had been present at the scene of the crime."

Sources close to the investigation have said a footprint at the scene was one of the few pieces of physical evidence police had found.

Randy Knight, the Kansas City man who authorities say killed a Springfield woman before he fled to Alaska, was ordered bound over for trial Wednesday.

Knight, 27, is charged with both second-degree murder and felony murder in the Nov. 2 shooting of Jamesetta Johnston, 31. He is also charged with armed criminal action and first-degree assault on James Scotten.

Knight had been returned to Springfield by Kansas City authorities after he was arrested there on a warrant. He had been working in Alaska as an automobile repair technician, a job he held in Springfield before fleeing.

Johnston's murder was the 12th in Springfield this year, the highest total recorded here in more than a decade.

An armed robbery and a high-speed chase from Forum Boulevard to Callaway County ended in the arrest Wednesday of a Wilkes-Barre man wanted for kidnapping and for parole violation.

Jeffrey Cole, 29, and a female accomplice are believed to have tried to rob Forum Dry Cleaners at 1114 I-70 Drive S.W. on Wednesday. Police said Cole pulled a gun and made an employee open the cash register; the two then fled with an undisclosed sum of cash. After pursuit by the Springfield and Callaway sheriffs' departments, Cole was caught in Callaway County.

After the bars close and the parties break up, the city's late-night eateries brace themselves for potentially obnoxious, often inebriated customers. But the customers usually don't carry sawed-off shotguns. And they usually don't empty the cash register.

At 1:46 a.m. Thursday, two men entered Country Kitchen Family Restaurant and did just that, to the horror of the five employees and five customers present. No shots were fired, and no one was hurt, police said.

Two men walked into the restaurant at 1712 N. Providence Road, flashed the shotgun and ordered everyone to lie down. With the help of an employee, one suspect removed the money from the register, then forced the employee to take him to the office to retrieve more money, said Police Capt. Dennis Veach.

Student Name _____ Course _____ Date_____

EXERCISE: ABBREVIATIONS AND ACRONYMS
Correct the style errors in the following sentences.

1. The U.S.-led peacekeeping mission restored peace in Bosnia.

2. K.O.M.U. is a commercial television station affiliated with N.B.C.

3. Adams is in a diving class taught by Tom Rainey, manager of Diver's Village, 131 S. 7th Street.

4. The measure was introduced by Senator Tom Harkin, D.-Iowa.

5. The ATR-72 crashed in a rainstorm while en route from Indianapolis to Chicago.

6. The F.B.I. said it would cooperate fully with the CIA.

7. He lives at Ninth and Elm streets in Peoria, Illinois.

8. Soldiers stayed on guard at Ft. Knox, and the gold supply remained secure.

9. The U.S. voted against the U.N. resolution condemning Israeli occupation of the land.

10. Roy Fenton, Jr., of 114 Pacific Avenue, said he will call Atty. Gen. Antonio Perez the next time he has a complaint.

11. The Tigers ended Oklahoma State's 15-year reign as No. 1 in the conference.

12. He said the Idaho Hospital Assn. would decide the issue next month.

13. Earl C. Bryden, 54, of 734 Demaret Dr., was the defendant.

14. He watched a documentary about the B1 bomber on TV.

15. She rode AMTRAK for the 1st time in 1996.

EXERCISE: CAPITALIZATION
Correct the style errors in the following sentences.

1. She ate the remains of a Waldorf salad, a few French fries, and drank a Manhattan cocktail.

2. Schneider has a Psychology degree he received last year from the university of Kansas.

3. The pope sent the President a message.

4. The Atlanta Braves signed Outfielder Jeff Francoeur to a multi-year contract.

5. According to Werner erhard, "the truth believed is a lie."

6. Mei-ling left the east after college and traveled west to realize her dreams in Hollywood.

7. The Associated Press stylebook is a journalist's Bible.

8. Burkino Fasso is a country in northwest Africa.

9. Tarzan, a 10-year-old Bassett Hound, disappeared Sunday.

10. Former president Bill Clinton worked for peace around the world.

11. The president said constitutional guarantees are sufficient and no legislation by Congress would help.

12. The Bangor city council will meet at 7 P.M. Monday.

13. The crime is a Federal offense.

14. Men from earth may visit Mars during the coming century.

15. The Rocky mountains are the highest in the United States.

16. George W. Bush was elected by the narrowest of margins.

17. The mayor said Accountant Chung Min-Lee was at fault.

18. "I'd walk a mile for a CAMEL," the sign read.

19. The Army buys Jeeps by the thousands.

20. Cassandra Solarz was named realtor of the year.

EXERCISE: PUNCTUATION AND HYPHENATION
Correct the style errors in the following sentences.

1. The Rev. Slidell Thomas, Jr., said he was certain that the incident had parallels to Jesus's life.

2. He conducted a post-mortem on the postdoctoral student.

3. The exconvicts' group meets once-a-month at the Presbyterian Church.

4. Elvis Presley was known to millions as the King of Rock 'n' Roll.

5. Teachers salaries should be competitive with those of other districts'.

6. He is the president of Smith Foods Co., Inc.

7. "Who's going to change the light bulb?," she asked.

8. Stephen Crane wrote "The Red Badge of Courage".

9. He was given a five- to 10-year prison sentence.

10. He is a first class fiddle player who is known throughout the area she said.

11. "For appearance's sake," he said, "We decided it would be better to hire an auditing firm.

12. The music he produces is played mostly on Mexican American stations.

13. "Music and art are important parts of education, he said. "Without them it would be a drab world."

14. Sven Swennson, 29, of Hays, Kan. was indicted.

15. "He said, "Throw it down", so I did."

EXERCISE: NUMERALS
Correct the style errors in the following sentences.

1. The Eighth U.S. Circuit Court of Appeals ruled that the case did not involve the 1st Amendment.

2. The $8,900,000 fund would be used to help farmers hurt by the drought.

3. The Detroit Red Wings beat the Boston Bruins 5 to 3.

4. He said the odds were 5-1 that the Braves would not repeat as champions.

5. Sunday's high will be about 29 degrees Fahrenheit.

6. Irving Malestrom, twenty-one, and Jill Solomon, 19, will be married on Jan. 19th.

7. He lives at 3,008 Paris Rd., which is in the 3rd Ward.

8. Housing costs are expected to soar more than ten per cent annually during the next decade.

9. 34 more students are expected to enroll this year.

10. 2004 was a very good year for the rock group.

11. The sermon should start about 10:00 a.m., he said.

12. Hancock's amendment would cut funding for the measure by 1/4.

13. He had received 3459 responses to the questionnaire by Sunday.

14. He is the number one student in a class of 153.

15. She said the value of a share of Apple Computer rose 1 1/4 points in less than 2 hours.

EXERCISE: GRAMMAR, SPELLING AND WORD USAGE
Correct the style errors in the following sentences.

1. The legislator said it was difficult deciding between the three candidates for gov.

2. The team (that was comprised of two men and seven women) won it's first game 6-2.

3. He said the fire began when someone lay some plastic parts too near the furnace. Before anyone noticed, he said, the blaze was well underway.

4. Farley said he didn't know whom among the teen-agers present at the time was involved in the theft.

5. "We don't have enough aides to accomodate all the patients," Reinhardt said.

6. Hopefully, the U.S. won't have to actually call up the men who registered for the draft, he said.

7. Welles said the city was looking for someone that is familiar with the kinds of problems Columbia faces and whom has several years experience as a City Manager.

8. "This Fall," Hendrick said, "the state should face up to the problem of toxic wastes, and pass stringent legislation against dumping them."

9. The committee's concensus was that less people would attend the festival this year as a result of the violence that marred it last year.

10. When the camper stopped, Simmons woke up and stepped out of the back to see what was wrong. But his wife Mary didn't know that, and drove off without him.

11. Shirley Richards fought in Vietnam, and her son fought in Iraq.

12. German Chancellor Angela Merkel and French President Nicolas Sarkozy agreed that the recent performance of the Euro has been a pleasant surprise.

Student Name _____ Course _____ Date_____

───

EXERCISE: STYLE
Correct the style errors in the following sentences.

1. Compton Packing Company will sell the meat immediately.

2. Jason Michlowski won the first set 6-3, but lost all the rest 6 to 0.

3. Al Roker is N.B.C.'s weather forecaster on the Today show.

4. Rigor in editing is essential, Prof. Ed Trayes insisted.

5. The University of Maine is ranked No. 1 in the nation.

6. The first meeting of the committee will be at 2 p.m., Sun., Jan. 26.

7. Sergeant First Class Bill Simpson has been assigned to an army outpost in Alaska.

8. Rev. Germaine Jones will lead the congregation in singing.

9. First National Bank is at Eighth and Broadway.

10. The Secretary of Defense said yesterday in Minneapolis the President will not make a decision before Feb. 1 at the earliest.

11. Houston, Texas, is one of the leading cities in the southwest.

12. Abbreviations of more than two letters usually do not require periods, but there are exceptions, including c.o.d.

13. He lives at 809 Springer Terr.

14. A buss is a vehicle and a bus is a kiss.

15. Communist Party leaders had hoped to make Communism a way of life in the country, but that goal ended with the collapse of the Berlin Wall.

EXERCISE: STYLE
Correct the style errors in the following sentences.

1. Stephen Harper, a conservative, was elected as prime minister of Canada.

2. The House ways and means committee will meet at 3 p.m. Friday to discuss the president's proposals.

3. Dr. John Kuhlheart, professor of economics at the University, will teach the course this semester.

4. The Rev. Mr. Monk Bryan served at First United Methodist Church before becoming a bishop.

5. First National Bank has lowered its prime interest rate to 5 per cent.

6. The Republican party has chosen San Diego, California for the site of it's convention.

7. An American Airlines DC9 limped into Midway Airport in Chicago after brushing a light aircraft above Belleville, Illinois.

8. Bob Pugh, ex-mayor, lives at 502 West Rock Creek Dr.

9. Many believe the U.S. should not contribute so much to N.A.T.O. now that the Warsaw Pact is gone.

10. The 6th US Circuit Court of appeals was expected to issue its decision in February, 1997.

11. Former U.S. Rep. Jerry Litton (D.-Mo.) was killed in a plane crash after winning the senatorial nomination.

12. The board of directors will meet Fri. in Cooperstown, New York.

13. Sen. Alice Rausch, D-New Hampshire, asked if the company had attempted to influence the dicision with a contribution of $3,800,000.

14. The Senate vote on the ammendment by Representative Locarno was 235 to 189.

15. The freshmen class is large, but not the largest in history.

EXERCISE: STYLE
Correct the style errors in the following sentences.

1. He was born in Boise, Idaho December 19, 1947 to the late John and Mary Beasley.

2. The last vote on the issue was in May 1991 when it was defeated by ten votes.

3. Atlanta, Ga., was the sight of the 1996 Olympics.

4. The United States Constitution provides that no president may seize control of the Armed Forces.

5. Mayor Darwin Hindman, First Ward Councilman Richard Lane and Fifth Ward Councilman Melinda Farhad voted against it

6. The Communist Party and the Socialist Workers party were unable to win spots on the state ballot.

7. The president said he will spend 2 days at Camp David, Md. preparing for his address to congress.

8. Ft. Benning, Ga. is the home of the infantry.

9. Over 3,000 students went to the polls, the campus newspaper reported.

10. Congress is trying to decide whether to fund more B-2 bombers.

11. Teenagers are to meet with the city council at 7 p.m. Monday.

12. The U.N. was the scene of the worst confrontation of U.S. and Russian diplomats in sixteen years.

13. Lawmen searched the five-country area, but were unable to find clues to the murder.

14. A 22 caliber pistol was used in the shooting, said Roger Robards, Sheriff.

15. Rep. Steny Hoyer, D-Maryland, is majority leader of the House.

16. High mass will be said at the church Sunday at 9 a.m., said the Most Rev. John Kelley, bishop.

EXERCISE: SENTENCE TIGHTENING
Edit the following sentences to eliminate verbosity.

1. A new graduate course in communications law is being introduced this semester.

2. The firm of Johnson & O'Reilly, Inc. entered a bid of $3,571.

3. Those who are majoring in environmental physiology are few in number.

4. All of a sudden the supply was exhausted.

5. For a period of 10 days, workers labored in excess of 12 hours daily to finish

the building.

6. Authorities are going to inform those in the immediate vicinity of the leak to evacuate.

7. In view of the fact that the cafe no longer accepts advance reservations, we can't eat there.

8. That bald-headed man is the father of a baby boy born Saturday.

9. The store is located at the corner of Ninth and Elm Streets in Springfield.

10. The show begins at 7 p.m. Sunday night in the auditorium.

11. Floodwaters entirely destroyed the city despite the fact that there was a floodwall around it.

12. Steve Miller said he was kicked off of the team, but the coach said he quit.

13. The appellate court remanded the case back to Boone County Circuit Court.

14. The president tendered his resignation after being confronted with the evidence.

15. Underground subways are common in New York and in some European cities.

16. Police said she was a self-confessed killer.

17. The odor of onion still persists because neither of you has taken out the garbage.

18. The CIA is an agency charged with foreign, not domestic, intelligence responsibilities.

19. The chairman received his education at Tulane University in New Orleans.

20. He was the husband of Anna Schaeffer, who died in the early 1990s, about 1992.

EXERCISE: SENTENCE TIGHTENING
Edit the following sentences to eliminate verbosity.

1. Police believe he was strangled to death.

2. It reverts back to the former subject.

3. She was met by a screaming throng of persons.

4. The man fell a distance of 50 feet.

5. A lightning bolt struck the house.

6. You could get into a movie then for the sum of 25 cents.

7. The meeting, which was held last night, began at 7:30 p.m. in the Municipal Building.

8. The company is engaged in the construction of several motels.

9. In the event that it rains, the game will be postponed.

10. A great number of times he's wrong.

11. The petition did not get a sufficient number of signatures.

12. The building was a flaming inferno.

13. A good firefighter leams to descend down the pole rapidly.

14. The car was moving with a rapid amount of speed.

15. In excess of 300 persons attended the show.

16. At the present time he is available.

17. Everyone, with the exception of Sheila, was included.

18. That city often gets snow during the winter months.

19. At the conclusion of the meeting it was obvious there was no agreement.

20. He was absolutely certain he could still sing.

EXERCISE: SPELLING
Circle the correctly spelled word in each pair.

1. accessable, accessible
2. accommodate, accomodate
3. acquit, aquit
4. adviser, advisor
5. athalete, athlete
6. baby sitter, baby-sitter
7. begining, beginning
8. bona fide, bonafide
9. concensus, consensus
10. defendant, defendent
11. dietician, dietitian
12. doughnut, donut
13. embarrass, embarrass
14. fire fighter, firefighter
15. grammar, grammer
16. guerilla, guerrilla
17. harass, harass
18. imposter, impostor
19. judgement, judgment
20. leisure, leisure
21. memento, momento
22. misspell, misspell
23. necessary, necessary
24. neice, niece
25. occasion, occassion

26. occured, occurred
27. OK, okay
28. paid, payed
29. parallel, parallel
30. pastime, past-time
31. precede, preceed
32. perogative, prerogative
33. piviledge, privilege
34. professor, professor
35. readable, readable
36. relevant, relevant
37. reknowned, renowned
38. restauranteur, restaurateur
39. rhythm, rythm
40. rock 'n' roll, rock 'n' roll
41. seige, siege
42. seize, sieze
43. supeney, subpoena
44. sophomore, sophmore
45. truely, truly
46. usable, useable
47. villain, villian
48. weird, wierd
49. wholely, wholly
50. woolen, woolen

Student Name _____ Course _____ Date_____
_____

EXERCISE: STORY EDITING
Edit this story as directed by your instructor.

ARSON

The Springfield Fire Department is investigating an arson that occurred early
Wednesday morning in the Woodland Hills Mobile Home Park on Blackfoot Road in
northwest Springfield.

Firefighters arrived at lot 54 just after 3 a.m. to find the vacant single-wide home
engulfed in flames. No one was injured, said department spokesman Steven Sapp.

Soon after firefighters extinguished the blaze, investigators determined it was set
intentionally.

"It looks like a random act of vandalism," Sapp said. "That's what most arsons are."

Damage is estimated at $2,000.

"The trailer was not an expensive piece of property," he said. "But this is still a
criminal investigation."

Sapp said the trailer was sold this week but the owner is not a suspect.

"It was not insured, so there'd be no reason for someone to burn it." he said.

EXERCISE: STORY EDITING
Edit this story as directed by your instructor.

PLANE

A pilot trapped in a smoke-filled cockpit safely landed a small private airplane at Springfield Regional Airport at about 10 p.m. Wednesday.

Airport officials would not release information about the pilot or his two passengers, but they did say all three people were uninjured.

Emergency vehicles scrambled to the airport at 9:50 p.m. after airport control received a report from Louisville International Airport that there was smoke in the cockpit of an incoming airplane.

The airplane, a modified twin-engine Piper Cheyenne, was more than five minutes from Springfield Regional Airport when the alert phone rang, giving safety officers time to prepare for the potential emergency.

"It was a precarious situation," said Millard Young, a public safety officer at the airport. "It's not like you can pull to one side of the road. . . . It was a good thing they were close to the airport."

Young inspected the plane after it landed. He said the smell of burned electrical insulation filled the cockpit. The plane was carrying 1,800 pounds of fuel. "I imagine it was well over half-full, probably full," Young said.

Emergency crews responded to about 178 alerts at the airport last year, he said. Most of them were the result of problems in private airplanes, which aren't inspected as often as commercial planes, Young said. The Federal Aviation Administration will investigate.

EXERCISE: STORY EDITING
Edit this story as directed by your instructor.

COCAINE

An argument about money between a 14-year-old juvenile and two adults ended in one arrest for suspicion of possession of crack cocaine and two for suspicion of kidnapping and assault.

According to Springfield police, the 14-year-old was walking with two friends on McBaine Avenue on Tuesday night when Michael Touchstone, 44, of 309 Washington Ave.and Penny Belliard, 34, of Centralia approached them in a truck.

Touchstone, Belliard and the boy began to argue about an unknown amount of money. But, according to police, the three have not said what the argument concerned and have not acknowledged knowing each other.

"There are very conflicting stories about the incident," said police Capt. Chris Egbert. "Between the three of them, they both know each other, and they don't."

After arguing for some time, Touchstone and Belliard allegedly threatened the 14-year-old and then threw him into their truck and drove away.

The two other youths stopped a passing patrol car. As they were reporting the incident, the truck drove by.

The police stopped the truck and arrested Touchstone and Belliard.

Egbert said while they checked the boy for injuries, one of the officers discovered "a few loose rocks of crack cocaine" in his possession.

He was arrested and turned over to juvenile authorities. Touchstone and Belliard were released from the Boone County Jail on $2,000 bond each.

Student Name _____ Course _____ Date_____
_____

EXERCISE: STORY EDITING
Edit this story as directed by your instructor.

INSURE

Auto theft in Springfield has decreased, but auto insurance premiums still may rise as a result of the 5 percent auto theft increase in the state, said the Highway Patrol and the Insurance Information Service.

In 1996, 142 vehicles were reported stolen in the city compared with 155 vehicles reported in 1991, said Springfield police Capt. Dennis Veach.

"It's not dramatically lower, but those are things we don't have a lot of control over," Veach said. "We've reached a specific level of theft and haven't greatly fluctuated from that in a number of years."

Springfield's clearance rate is more than 22 percent. This rate compares the number of cars recovered and arrests of the thieves with the number of stolen vehicles.

"The vast majority of our vehicles are recovered in near or same condition as it was stolen," Veach said. "But occasionally we run into pros who take them into chop shops and strip them."

Springfield's good fortune, however, does mean that city residents are safe from the cost of the 23,735 vehicles reported stolen in the state last year.

"Auto theft continues to be a big business in the state and motorists are paying for it," said Calvin Call, executive director of the Insurance Information Service.

Auto thefts, as any other claims, will eventually increase the overall cost of auto insurance premiums, said insurance officials.

The auto theft increases mean the state's motorists are paying nearly $124 million, based on an estimate of $5,222 per stolen vehicle, Call said.

"The consumer buying auto insurnce has to be concerned with one of two things," he said. "One, that their car is a potential target. Two, anytime insurance has to pay out more dollars in claims the more they have to collect in premiums, causing insurance prices to rise."

The state's increase in auto theft is attributed mostly to big-city figures. Chicago police reported a 14 percent rise in stolen vehicles.

Locally, car theft, at an average of three reported a week, is not a big business, Veach said.

"Most are stolen for the ride, not to resale parts or such," Veach said.

EXERCISE: STORY EDITING
Edit this story as directed by your instructor.

OUSLER

Cynthia Ousler likes to cook, spend time with her cat and watch the World Series. But her true passion is reading. She's read almost everything from mysteries to baseball books.

Ousler, 91, is now rereading the complete works of William Shakespeare. She began last summer with "King John" and is now into "Henry V." She usually reads from her Shakespeare volume during the dinner hour, sitting in her most comfortable chair, savoring each word.

"Reading it again the way I'm reading it — critically and two scenes at a time — is probably the best way in the world," Ousler says.

She should know. From the '40s to the '70s, when she was an instructor at Knox College in Illinois, Ousler taught Shakespeare, mythology, classical literature and Greek.

Although Ousler says Shakespeare is one of her favorite writers, "I'm not reading with stars in my eyes. Some people think Shakespeare's almost holy. I think people have made a mistake in putting Shakespeare on a pedestal, worshipping him instead of reading him as a very successful playwright."

Ousler recalls a card game called Shakespeare she played as a child. An illustration appeared on each card with a quote from the play. Players were expected to read the quote, then identify the play, act and scene.

The lovely illustrations and language captured her interest. She thinks the world would be a better place if everyone read Shakespeare.

"It's like having a child and not ever letting him eat ice cream — just a plain shame," she says. "Ice cream doesn't do anything for his health or well-being, but there is the pleasantness of the taste of ice cream.

"The same thing is true of Shakespeare."

EXERCISE: STORY EDITING
Edit this story as directed by your instructor.

TAXHIKE

On Tuesday, you will be asked to make an $11.1 million choice.

If your answer is yes, the city will tack on a quarter-cent to your sales taxes for the next five years.

And, for your contribution to the $11.1 million, you will receive a new downtown fire station, an expanded police and joint communications headquarters, streets and sidewalk repairs and some undeveloped land to buffer the Nature Nature/Fitness Trail. The list goes on.

"We have to keep the city in good shape, and to do that requires a diversity of public improvements," said Fourth Ward Councilman Rex Campbell. "The past bond issues have only been for streets. Now it's time to go beyond that."

No one is prepared to say what happens if you answer no. City officials have not discussed alternate means of funding these projects. Instead they say the tax is important to maintain "quality of life," a much bandied-about, but ill-defined, slogan.

City politicians have crossed their fingers that voters will make what they consider the right choice.

But local attorney William Samuels and his group, rallying under the name Citizens Against Unfair Taxation, say the right choice is "no."

Richard Catlett, a member of the group, said the economy does not need a tax increase and that some of the projects should be funded separately instead of under an omnibus measure.

The Nature Trail and the joint communications system, Catlett said, are worth funding, but the whole package is not worth it. "They've got some cheesecake in there that they don't need in a sales tax." he said.

With a backlog of more than $25 million in capital improvement projects awaiting funding, council members have spent the better part of three years deciding on priorities.

"If you've got your choice in the general fund budget for a new fire engine or a soccer field, what are you going to choose?" Third Ward Councilman Bob Hutton said. "There are some things we can live without, but there are some things that are very important." He targeted public safety as the neediest area. The last time the city raised money for street improvements was 1985.

If passed, Springfield's sales tax rate would not change. The city's increase would go into effect July 1, the day the county's 1998 quarter-cent sales tax increase to fund the courthouse renovations and new jail expires.

EXERCISE: STORY EDITING
Edit this story as directed by your instructor.

JOURNALS

The Handbook of Organic Chemistry has been a staple of the Springfield University library system's reference section since 1918. Last year the subscription to this multi-volume set was cancelled. The reason: Its $20,000 price tag.

While most serials are neither as large nor as pricey as the chemistry handbook, their costs have doubled over the past five years, causing serious problems for research libraries across the country.

Combine sky-high subscription rates with an acquisitons budget at the University has failed to keep pace with inflation, and you have a recipe for hand-wringing, head-holding and, ultimately, cancellations. Libraries are the engine rooms of academia and journals are the tools researchers and students rely on to churn out new knowledge and forge discoveries. Without these tools of the trade, work slows and learning suffers.

Last year, 877 journal titles were cancelled in response to a $200,000 shortfall in the serials budget. An additional 210 titles were cut to allow for subscriptions to 255 new publications. This year, administrators face a shortfall of $233,000.

Martha Alexander, M.U. director of libraries, hopes university officials will reallocate funds to prevent elimination of more titles. Still, she is preparing for the worst and has asked departments to identify serials for potential cancellation totaling $250,000.

The women's studies department has yet to prepare its "hit list" since the choices now are so difficult, said Sharon Welch, the department's director.

She said the department already has cut to the bone.

"We're now having to look at the established journals, ones that are widely recognized and cited. It's a crisis in terms of our ability to provide the information we need for faculty to do research and for students to do term papers."

Bob Bauer, associate professor of geology and chair of the Campus Library Committee of Faculty, Staff and Students, said journal cancellations are of particular concern in the sciences, where research is generated rapidly and prices are often higher. The average price of a science serial subscription is $500 to $1,000, he said.

The percentage of the university's budget in support of libraries also has dropped. In 1971, the library and its branches received 4.1 percent of the University's total budget. By 2003, that dropped to 2.3 percent.

Those costly titles are what Douglas Randall, associate professor of biochemistry, describes as "the newspapers of our world." Without ready access to the latest news, the work can't be done efficiently, he said.

"Journals are probably the most efficient means of information transfer we have. You don't have to reinvent the wheel. What someone has learned on disease X might be vital to your own research on disease Y."

Clark Gantzer, associate professor in the school of natural resources, said this year his department had to drop a journal that is "essential to our field."

Gantzer said journal cancellations are tough on individual departments and reflect badly on the university in general. "If you're a first-rate university, you've got to have journals. Let's face it, one of the main criteria of a major institution is its holdings."

Since 1978, the library has suffered a steady decline in its national rating. In that year, it had the 35th largest collection among the nation's 107 research libraries. By 2003, that ranking had dropped to 46th, according to the Association of Research Libraries.

EXERCISE: STORY EDITING
Edit this story as directed by your instructor.

ABUSE

Teresa Byars has seen a lot in her 44-year life.

She is a mother of five. She has worked her way through college as an adult, and she has walked out on jobs that didn't pay enough. Currently, she volunteers at a shelter for battered women and has a part-time job at a rehabilitation center.

Byars has also been a victim of domestic abuse. She has been verbally and emotionally harassed; she has been slapped and choked and violently shaken; she's been thrown against walls; she's been sexually assaulted; and she's been threatened with death.

But Byars' story is one of hope — a story that proves women can break the cycle of domestic violence and sexual assault when they are armed with the knowledge of what constitutes domestic abuse and can recognize how and when to get out of a bad situation.

The Coalition Against Domestic Violence reports that about 4 million women are severely assaulted by their male partners each year in the U.S. Closer to home, 4,475 women were sheltered by the coalition's member programs last year, an increase of 22% in one year.

In Springfield alone, The Shelter, a program for victims of domestic violence and sexual assault, answered more than 13,000 phone calls about incidents of domestic violence in 1997, said Karen Johnson, coordinator of volunteer services at The Shelter.

"It's a holocaust," Johnson said. "It's different from a war because it's men that say I love you while they're doing it. And they kill us and they rape us and they batter us and they say I love you while they're doing it."

Byars would likely agree with that assessment.

When she was a teen-ager, she became part of an abusive cycle that lasted for the better part of 20 years and three husbands. In 1972, when she was 18, Byars married a man four years her senior. They were both young and immature. Though the marriage lasted five years and included the birth of two children, it was fraught with problems.

Her husband, who was an alcoholic, verbally and emotionally abused her. The marriage ended in 1977, and Byars moved from Jackson, Miss., to Columbus, Miss., in February 1979 to distance herself and her children from her ex-husband. She met a man two years later whom she married after a short time.

Her second husband did not physically assault her - at first. He was, however, mentally and emotionally abusive.

"He constantly threatened to leave me," Byars said. "In fact, he did about every other day — he walked out on me."

She had a third child — a son — with this husband, and when she became pregnant with her fourth child, the relationship with her husband deteriorated. He accused her of having an affair and said the child was not his.

The emotional stress took its toll on Byars during the pregnancy.

"I went into premature labor at seven months because of all the harassment."

After she gave birth, Byars divorced her husband. It was 1983. That same year, she met another man, her "knight in shining armor," and they were married.

The cycle of violence that had been a part of her life for the previous 11 years appeared to have been broken. The man had a good job at a wallpaper plant. He would be a good provider for her children. He studied the Bible. She had another daughter.

However, as she soon discovered, the worst was yet to come. Six months into the marriage, her husband blew up at her. He had knocked over some of Byars' wine decanters after she had continually asked him to be careful. When she became upset, he blamed her.

"He said, 'It's not my fault," Byars recalled. "'You put them in my way. You're the reason I broke them. If you hadn't done it, it never would've happened.' "

This type of behavior — redirecting the blame toward the victim — is common in abusive people, said The Shelter's Johnson.

The way Byars' husband reacted later that day is typical of abusive personalities as well. Although he never apologized for his verbal assault, Byars said he was kind and loving to her that evening.

As time passed, though, the abuse increased. Byars' husband began drinking and smoking marijuana regularly. The children irritated him. He told Byars she was fat. He forced her to have sex against her will and told her that if she left he would kill her.

"You've heard things about domestic violence," Byars said. "And I would think, you know, I don't know why these women don't just get up and walk out."

But it's not always that simple.

"I guess it was something that just kept building and building, and I kept feeling like I was drowning," Byars said. "And I knew something had to be done. I knew I had to get out."

Byars asked her husband to leave on Labor Day 1989. She was left with no job and five children to raise. She scraped by for a time, working at a $4.75-an-hour secretarial job and receiving some child support from her former husbands. She was not able to collect food stamps because she and her husband owned a van that was worth more than $14,000.

Byars says the family got by "by the grace of God." Eventually, her husband came back. After about nine months of being apart, he began taking Byars out to dinner occasionally. He sent her flowers. He finally agreed to counseling. The counseling did not last long, however. Nor did the everyday niceties.

Once, when Byars refused to have sex, he pulled out his .38 revolver and forced her. He told her how he'd like to stone her to death.

After an incident during Labor Day weekend in 1991, Byars gave her husband an ultimatum: He would have to leave or she would leave, with the children, and go to a shelter. This time he left again — for good. Byars was finally granted a divorce in June 1992.

Since then, Byars' life has been a roller-coaster ride of emotions. Despite being taken to court several times by her second husband, she was able to earn her bachelor's degree in criminal justice from the University of Mississippi. At Ole Miss, Byars started dating a graduate student in the classics department.

They are now happily married, and Byars is pursuing her master's degree in criminal justice at the University and volunteering at the Springfield Police Department. Her husband is studying for his doctoral degree in classics at the University.

Her youngest daughter, who is 13, lives at home with Byars in Springfield. Her oldest daughter is a teacher; her second oldest is nearly finished with college and plans to attend seminary. Her 16-year-old son and a 15-year-old daughter live with their father, Byars' second husband.

As for Byars, she has moved on. But her past will be a part of her for the rest of her life.

"I look back and part of me is the same person, but part of me is not," Byars said. "Ten years ago, I never would've dreamed that I would be here now."

7

Holistic Editing: Integrating the Macro and the Micro

QUIZ: HOLISTIC EDITING OVERVIEW
Circle T for true or F for false.

T F   1. Writers of local-history pieces should make up descriptions and quotes when historically accurate ones are not available in order to make the story read well.

T F   2. The "Wall Street Journal formula" is a feature-story organization that analyzes an abstract issue and starts by showing how it affects a particular person.

T F   3. Personality profiles should present selective, themed details.

T F   4. Two of the most common problems with sports features are use of clichés and needless insertion of opinion, but there also seems to be greater acceptance of these in sports features than in other kinds.

T F   5. The two most common angles for a featurized obit include a distinguishing characteristic or achievement of the deceased that serves as a summing up of that person's life.

T F   6. Q-and-A formats should be used only readers would likely prefer seeing more of the person's words quoted in full than reading a more selective, arranged and descriptive account.

T F   7. In multiple-interview features, it's especially important to make sure attributions are clear.

T F   8. Seasonal features can be regularly counted on for page-filling ideas, but the trick is to say something original in them.

T F   9. A trick to remember about "color pieces" is to avoid overusing modifiers.

T F   10. The term "human-interest story" is often used as a synonym for feature, but it refers more specifically to a story focusing on an unusual or emotionally involving event.

T F   11. "Service journalism" is always written in the "how-to" format.

T F   12. You're legally protected when running a bad review even if you get a few facts wrong.

T F   13. Accident, court and crime stories have in common that editors must make sure no one is convicted in the media before a verdict is announced.

T F   14. Food stories, like sports stories, tend to use numerals for fractions and single-digit numbers, contrary to usual wire-service style.

T F   15. Two major problems with political stories are bias and covering campaigns as horse races rather than the issues.

T F   16. When covering wars, make sure you take the side of the country in which the media outlet you report for is located so as not to alienate your audience.

T F   17. In covering a weather story about a storm, remember that the "eye" is the most turbulent part, not the calmest.

T F   18. Any non-mainstream religion is a "cult."

T F   19. For precision, medical terms should not be translated into common English.

B. Put the letter of the best answer in front of the number of the question.

____20. Science and health stories may commonly be written as features by:
a. focusing on a researcher
b. analyzing a new development and what it means
c. taking a how-to approach
d. ALL OF THE ABOVE

____21. When turning a press release into an advance feature, you should do all BUT which of the following?
a. Get rid of self-serving, self-promoting, nonobjective language.
b. Make sure the focus is on what the readers might find interesting, not merely what the sponsor wants to say.
c. Run it "as is" so as not to offend a possible advertiser.
d. Consider turning it into a personality profile of a key person involved or a historical piece about the person or group, while teasing the news peg event in the story or taking the time-day-place and cost details out and putting them into a box.

____22. Travel pieces are often hurt by:
a. lack of the Wall Street Journal formula
b. overuse of dangling participles
c. use of clichés and overuse of description
d. not enough human interest

____23. When editing someone else's features, some useful advice includes all BUT which of the following?
a. Allow the reporter more leeway to be personally creative as opposed to objective and impersonal.
b. Allow yourself more time to edit them and to come up with more creative headlines.
c. Be aware that features often have more sidebars, pictures, second-deck headlines and so forth to coordinate.
d. To make features fit a limited space, cut them from the bottom like any other kind of story.

____24. Business features are often hurt by:
a. unexplained figures and focus on things rather than people
b. a pro-management perspective
c. use of clichés and overuse of description
d. lack of a strong ending

____25. Common problems with "how-to" features include all BUT which of the following?
a. the writer-as-expert approach when the writer isn't
b. the source as expert approach
c. unclear directions
d. technical jargon that's not explained

Student Name _____ Course _____ Date_____

EXERCISE: STORY EDITING
Edit the following story as directed by your instructor.

BRIDGE

The bridge on Southland Drive will be closed today between the hours of 8 in the morning to 5 in the evening while county crews replace boards on its deck.

Southland Drive runs between U.S. 63 South and Parkhurst St. in Springfield County. The bridge spans Swan Creek.

Dave Mosely, Sprimgfield Public Works Director, said the work was "strictly maintenance" and would take just the day. He said the bridge is one of only 6 plank bridges left in the county.

EXERCISE: STORY EDITING (PRESS RELEASE)
Edit the following press release as it might be received from the Springfield Consumer Mall into a news story that might run in the local Springfield newspaper:

MALL

Come one, come all to the Springfield Consumer Mall!!! We have the largest selection of merchandise under one roof in the Springfield area. And this weekend, we also have a large selection of health-care services available free to people who come in! The Mall will be holding its First Annual Health Fair Friday through Sunday during the Mall's regular hours. (10-9 Monday-Friday, 12 noon-9 Saturday, and 12 noon-6 Sunday). And it's all FREE!!! Dieticians will be on hand to hand out free pamphlets on eating healthy optometrists will give free eye exams; nurses will take your blood pressure and give away free colon-rectal cancer check kits and chiropractors will check your spine.

EXERCISE: STORY EDITING (OBITUARY)
Edit the following story as directed by your instructor.

YEARGIN OBIT

Marge N. Yeargin, 82, of Rural Route 7, passed away Saturday at Springfield County Hospital.

Mrs. Yeargin, was born February 12, 1936 in Newark, New Jersey to Joseph O. and Essie Lou Reed Johnson. She married Ross O. Yaergin on Jan. 27, 1959 in Kansas City. He preceded her in death.

Ms. Yeargin was active in the Springfield County League of Woman Voters for the last fifteen years. She also was member of the Springfield Baptist Church.

Survivors include three sons: Jesse B. yeargin, of Denver, Colorado; Russell B. Yeargin of 3435 East Willow St., and Howard R. Yeargin, Route 9, Two daughters Mrs. Willie Mayo, Route 9, and Mary Yeargin, of the home, and two grandchildren. A sister and brother preceded her in death also.

Services for Mrs. Yeargin will be at 2:00 Thursday afternoon at the Springfield Baptist Church, with Rev. Alfred Orr officiating. Burial will be completed at Oakland Cemetary.

Friends may call at Parkers Chapel any time Thursday prior to the service.

EXERCISE: STORY EDITING (FEATURE OBITUARY)
Edit the following story as directed by your instructor.

JEFFERS OBIT

Ben Jeffers had a city in his basement.

Jeffers himself built all the houses, factories, schools, churches, even the farm buildings in the surrounding countryside. He also built the roads and laid the train track connecting them all. It was a 27 year project for the model railroader, who died May 25, 2008 of a heart attack at age 62.

"Ben loved playing with his trains and building a little world around them," said Fran Jeffers, his wife. "He told me once that one of his first memories of life was traveling with his father on a train to Chicago."

Visititation will be held from 6-9 PM tonight at the Knapp Funeral Home, 1311 High Street in Springfield. Services will be 10 a.m. tomorrow at St. Joseph Catholic Church, with Fr. Jack DeMilo officiating, followed by burial in the church graveyard.

Born July 22, 1946 in Springfield, Ben married his wife Fran Sparrow on Aug. 10, 1974, and was a devoted husband and father for 34 years. He will be greatly missed.

He was a 1973 graduate of Springfield High School and member of St. Joseph's Catholic Church and Springfield Model Railroaders.

He was preceded in death by his parents, Oliver and Eileen Jeffers, and two older sisters, Abigail and Annette.

Survivors include his son Bill, 2340 Carleton Rd., Springfield, and daughter Mrs. Alan (Ellen) Hastings, 67429 Pitt Dr. in Jackson, MI and five grandchildren, Bill Jr., Tony, Jennifer, Charlene, and Jill. No flowers are wanted by the family.

EXERCISE: STORY EDITING (COURT STORY)
Edit this story as directed by your instructor.

COCAINE

Robert Yardley, 20, of Springfiled, was sentenced on Thursday in St. Louis to 2 years in federal prison without the possibility of parole for conspiring to distribute crack cocaine,

Yardley also must remain on probation for four years after he is released from prison.

In June, Yardley and James Warren, 19, also of Springfield, were arrested after they sold 7 ounces of crack to an undercover officer at the Drury Inn. They earlier had purchased the drugs from Isaac Martin, who turned himself into police.

All three men pleaded guilty on Sept. 1 during hearings before U.S. District Judge Scott Wright.

Yardley admitted that he and Martin traveled numerous times to Houston in April and May to buy cocaine. Yardely transported the drugs to Springfield, where he sold crack and powder cocaine.

Warren remains free on $25,000 bond, while Martin is being held without bond in the Cole County Jail. Sentencing dates for the two men have not been set.

EXERCISE: STORY EDITING (MEETING STORY)
Edit the following story as directed by your instructor.

IMPORT

The Springfield County Commission Friday denied 2-1 a rezoning request that would have allowed an import company to build a 70,000-square-foot retail outlet on Hartsburg Road.

But the project will go ahead in another location despite the setback,said Kay Lambrecht, a Springfield realtor representing the import company.

"It'll go – if I have my way" and possibly still in Springfield County, she said.

The company, which 23 investors have formed under the name Bring Home the World, will sell crystal, china, pottery, baskets, and furniture. Plans call for the company to hire 50 employees at opening, then up to 150 within a year.

Ms. Lambrecht said the Hartsburg Road sight was only one of eight possible ones in the state, including two more in Springfield.

The operation would be modeled on two similar businesses on the east coast at Williamsbvurg, VA and Myrtle Beach, SC.

But may residents in the Hartsburg Road area were less than enthusiastic, with thity-six signing a petition oppositing the development, which they presnted to the Springfield County Commission Sept. 27.

Chris Frech, of 8506 Hartsburg presented the arguments against the development to the Commission. She said the business was inappropriate for the agricultural area and might open the door to further development in the area.

Student Name _____ Course _____ Date_____

EXERCISE: STORY EDITING (CRIME STORY)
Edit the following story as directed by your instructor.

ARSON

Springfield Police announced today that they have issued a warrant for the arrest of Arlen McFarland, the owner of O'Malley's Irish Tavern in the downtown for arson in the fire that destroyed his bar the early hours of Friday before it opened.

When police went to his house to try to arrest him this morning, they found McFarland had fled.

Springfield Prosecuting Attorney Barbara Kettinger said today, Tuesday, March 17, that a small-time criminal from Osage, who is out on bond awaiting trial in an arson case there, told police last night he was angry that McFarland didn't pay him all of the $20,000 he had promised him to set the fire, so he decided to come forward and implicate him.

Kettinger granted Welch immunity from prosecution in this case in return for his testimony.

"It was an insurance scam, said Police Chief Irma Nelson. "McFarland payed Welch to torch his bar because business wasn't going well and he wanted out."

Police had earlier arrested a different man in the case, Bruce Villegas, but he was released without charges when the new evidence came in. Nelson said Villegas had been seen near the bar the night before the fire, and he had "naturally been a suspect" because he had previously been arrested for arson.

The fire at O'Malley's gutted the building, causing an estimated $1,200,000 dollars in damages.

EXERCISE: STORY EDITING (FEATURE STORY)
Edit the following story as directed by your instructor.

CHARITY

If the Good Samaritan had been criticized when he stopped to help, he might have felt like Dan Whitman.

"It demoralizes the hell out of you."

Whitman is the Springfield fire fighter who has been living in the back of a 1939 fire engine since 12 noon of Aug. 20. By confining himself in the 4'X8' area, he hoped to publicize the Muscular Dystophy fundraising drive sponsored by the Springfield firemen.

But Whitman has gotten both more and less than he hoped for.

The less is that so far the stunt has raised only about $2,000 -- $3,000 short of the $5,000 he hoped to raise.

The more part is worse: A local radio station reported Monday that the firefighters fund-raising effort may be illegal under the state's lottery law.

"It blows my mind," Whitman said. "It makes me feel like I'm Al Capone or something. If the police want to throw me in the clink, I'm use to the small space anyway."

State law prohibits the running of lotteries. A lottery is defined by statue as "an unlawful gambling scheme in which for a consideration the participants are given an opportunity to win something of value, the award of which is determined by chance."

The firemen are offering to those who contribute one dollar to the Muscular Dystrophy Association a chance to win a three-day trip to two to Las Vegas. The question is: Does that constitute an illegal lottery?

State attorney general Pete LaRoche said that as a rule charitable raffles are technically lotteries, but that enforcement varies from one area of the state to the next. In one district, the local sheriff even arrested a local Catholic priest for holding bingo nights.

Some states allow charities to apply for a special permit, but ours does not.

Springfield Prosecutor Fred Warren said this particular case falls into a gray area because the firefighters "have couched this as a contribution."

Further, he said, "No one has filed a complaint, and I have trouble seeing who the victim is. I don't think we need to come down on the fire department to save the morals of the county."

8

Writing Headlines, Titles, Captions and Blurbs

Student Name _____ Course _____ Date_____

QUIZ: WRITING HEADLINES, TITLES, CAPTIONS AND BLURBS
Circle T or F to indicate if the statement is true or false.

T F   1. Headlines, titles and blurbs are called "display type" and are designed to attract the reader's attention.

T F   2. Those who write compelling headlines are valued members of the newspaper staff.

T F   3. The best headlines keep the reader in suspense, even on a hard news story.

T F   4. A good headline depicts the mood of a story.

T F   5. The average reader does not read the average newspaper story.

T F   6. People who read a story in its entirety are less likely to find fault with it.

T F   7. When you write a headline, it's best to assume that the reader will not read the story.

T F   8. *USA Today* is probably the newspaper best in tune with how readers read.

T F   9. Good headline writers seldom learn the key-word method.

T F   10. Downstyle headlines are less common in newspapers than they were 50 years ago.

T F   11. There are no rules for writing headlines. Anything goes.

T F   12. Double-meaning headlines are funny and attract attention.

T F   13. Downstyle headlines are less common in newspapers than they were 50 years ago.

T F   14. Headlines should always be written in the future tense.

T F   15. Headlines should always be cute.

T F   16. It is impossible to commit libel in a headline.

T F   17. Blurbs are pullouts from stories placed in headline-sized type.

T F   18. Cutlines are multi-line captions.

T F   19. Magazines are more likely to call headlines "titles."

T F   20. Almost all of the conventions of headline writing apply equally well for the Internet.

PROBLEMS: WRITING THE NEWSPAPER HEADLINE

1. Analyze the headlines on the front page of your local newspaper. Explain how well you believe they accomplish the purposes of headlines.

2. Take the headline that you consider to be the worst on that page and rewrite it, using the same unit count. Explain why your headline is better.

3. Using newspapers available to you, identify and clip out an example of a headline with a kicker, with a secondary deck or dropout, and a hammer head. Tell whether you believe those headline forms were good choices for the stories on which they were used.

4. Read the headlines in an issue of your local newspaper. Then explain whether those headlines were sufficient to serve as an index to the day's news. Why or why not?

EXERCISE: COUNTING HEADLINES
Check your ability to determine headline unit counts by listing the count of each line in the space provided. Your instructor will specify the counting method to be used.

Fewer farms ____

supplying most ____

of our food needs ____

Doctors report ____

breakthrough ____

in AIDS testing ____

Mayor challenges ____

education leaders ____

to perform better ____

Mayor becomes ____

first to disclose ____

personal finances ____

Queen to honor ____

Nelson Mandela ____

at state dinner ____

Social Security ____

changes to affect ____

few in Delaware ____

Senate committee ____

to set conditions ____

for aid to junta ____

Germany wins ____

World Cup bid ____

over Australia ____

Braves' Glavine ____

allows Dodgers ____

lone hit in first ____

IBM stock rises ____

on announcment ____

of new processor ____

Teen gangs meet ____

to discuss truce ____

in bitter battle ____

Boating accidents ____

on area's rivers ____

at all-time high ____

EXERCISE: COUNTING HEADLINES

Check your ability to determine headline unit counts by listing the count of each line in the space provided. Your instructor will specify the counting method to be used.

Senate approves ____   **Virginia upsets** ____
mid-year raise ____   **Duke to capture** ____
for U.S. judges ____   **fourth ACC title** ____

Dow average ____   **Miami police raid** ____
losses largest ____   **drug warehouses** ____
in two months ____   **in center of city** ____

Sooners set sights ____   **Gay man chosen** ____
on national title ____   **to lead small city** ____
after banner year ____   **in central Iowa** ____

Lithuanian man ____   **Apple's iMac wins** ____
wins presidency ____   **award for design** ____
of U.N. panel ____   **at technical show** ____

Tiger Woods set ____   **Voters to choose** ____
to defend title ____   **best commercials** ____
this weekend ____   **in Europe, U.S.** ____

Taxes to increase ____   **Deadly chemical** ____
on steel imports ____   **found abandoned** ____
unless EU blinks ____   **at local warehouse** ____

Student Name _____ Course _____ Date_____
_____

PROBLEMS: HEADLINE WRITING
List the key words, those that must be included in the headline, for these leads.

1. A Muskegon man went berserk today in South Dearborn and shot and killed a boy getting off a school bus near his home.

2. Postal workers said Friday they would strike at midnight Sunday unless the government increases its pay offer to them.

3. The president of Burkina Fasso on Tuesday will become the first head of an African state to be honored with a state dinner since the new administration took office.

4. A Sacramento couple set a world speed-skating record on Thursday by skating uninterrupted for 87 hours.

EXERCISE: HEADLINE WRITING
Write headlines for these articles as specified by your instructor. Do not edit the stories.

SAMESEX

WASHINGTON (AP) – Legislation that would deny any federal sanction to same-sex marriages is getting low-priority treatment in the Senate despite its easy passage in the House and the president's endorsement.

The 342-67 House vote Friday followed a spirited debate in which proponents argued that it was essential to douse the "flames of hedonism" that Rep. Bob Barr, R-Ga., said are "licking at the very foundations of our society, the family unit."

Critics contended that the bill – the Defense of Marriage Act – scapegoats homosexuals for problems of traditional marriages.

BOMBING

HOSTAGES

ZAMBOANGA, Philippines (AP) — Extremists who grabbed 21 hostages from a diving resort a week ago issued written demands Saturday, while a journalist who saw the captives said they were being held in a small, island hut in squalid conditions and were poorly fed.

Meanwhile, troops who stormed the rebel group's stronghold on another Philippine island, Basilan, were unable to find a separate group of 27 hostages, including many children, who have been held for six weeks.

On Sulu island, the kidnappers, members of the Abu Sayyaf extremist group, presented a list of demands for the release of the 21 hostages, almost half of whom are foreign tourists, said Jamasali Abdurahman, a Muslim religious leader serving as a go-between.

SUSSEX

SUSSEX, Wis. (AP) – Parents were aghast: Sex had come to Sussex.

This village outside Milwaukee fielded complaining calls from parents of young children Friday after painters stopped work after only painting the letters 'SEX' on one side of a community water tower.

About a half dozen people called to complain, village administrator Chris Swartz said.

"There were more calls than we usually get on a village issue," he said. "They were asking how they could explain it to their children if they asked."

The painters completed the three letters Thursday, and, after a Friday morning rain let up, they added the "SUS."

"I wish in hindsight they would have started with the 'SUS,'" Swartz said.

SILVERSTONE

NEW YORK (AP) – As her first duty as producer of "Excess Baggage," Alicia Silverstone wanted to fire herself from the starring role.

"But they didn't go for that," says the 26-year-old "Clueless" star.

Because she was producing and starring, Silverstone wasn't sure she would be "good as an actress."

Silverstone is co-producing the action-adventure film – the first in her $10 million, two-picture deal with Columbia.

The studio's president of worldwide production, Barry Josephson, has credited her with hand-picking the cast.

ORPHAN

LAKEWOOD, Colo. (AP) — It is one of the least-remembered of America's migrations to the West: as many as 350,000 orphan children shipped out of New York on ``Orphan Trains" from the 1850s to 1929.

The trains stopped in rural areas so that prospective parents could look over the youngsters and decide whether to take in any of them.

The process wasn't always successful, recalled Dorothy Sharpley, 81, one of six Orphan Train ``riders" who attended a reunion Saturday in Colorado. Sharpley said she was rejected by her first adoptive family, in Columbus, Neb.

``I was sent back to New York only to ride the train again and end up in St. Mary's, Neb., only 20 miles from Columbus."

SLAVE

WASHINGTON (AP)—The U.S. Chamber of Commerce will solicit donations from U.S. corporations to compensate slave laborers who were forced to work in German factories owned by American companies or their subsidiaries during World War II, authorities said Saturday.

The chamber, which represents more than 3 million businesses worldwide, decided to establish the fund after being approached by the Clinton administration and a number of major U.S. corporations that have been threatened with lawsuits by survivors and their heirs.

Several U.S. corporations, including Ford and General Motors, have acknowledged having benefited from slave labor in the war.

EXERCISE: HEADLINE WRITING
Write headlines for these articles as specified by your instructor. Do not edit the stories.

BELFAST

BELFAST, Northern Ireland (AP) – Police exchanged gunfire in an IRA stronghold early today with gasoline bomb-throwing rioters who were venting their anger over traditional Protestant marches through Catholic neighborhoods.

Rioting and burning and hijacking of vehicles were reported for a second night in other Catholic districts of Belfast, in Londonderry,. Northern Ireland's second-largest city, and in several other towns.

The province's minority Catholics resent a police decision to allow two Protestant marches through Catholic districts Thursday and Friday. The Orange Order, the dominant Protestant fraternal group in Northern Ireland, marches throughout the province every July to celebrate its 17th century victories over Catholics.

GRIEF

PITTSBURGH (AP) – Even in Mr. Rogers' neighborhood, sometimes the days aren't so beautiful.

Fred Rogers, the star of PBS' "Mister Rogers' Neighborhood," choked up Wednesday as he talked about the loss of his father.

"There's a grief center inside all of us," Rogers said at a news conference to announce that he would be the chairman of the Pittsburgh Center for Grieving Children.

The center seeks to help children deal with the loss of loved ones.

Rogers said the pain young children feel when dealing with death is an issue that has been ignored.

HANGED

COVINGTON, Ky. (AP) – A man who taunted police for their inability to catch him, and then pleaded guilty to robbing 19 banks when he was apprehended, has hanged himself in his jail cell, authorities said.

Richard Lee Guthrie Jr. admitted robbing banks in seven states, including Missouri and Kansas. He sometimes wore shirts and hats with FBI logos. He left real and fake explosives at the scenes of some robberies and sent sarcastic letters to newspapers.

Guthrie, 38, who was from Baltimore, was arrested Jan. 15 in Green Township, in suburban Cincinnati, and pleaded guilty to federal bank robbery charges July 3.

AIRFARES

DALLAS (AP) – Major airlines have dropped the cost of flying many routes across the Midwest and the West Coast to just $75, taking some airfares down to less than 2 cents a mile.

To commemorate its anniversary, Southwest Airlines announced the $75 sale Friday, prompting United and American to match the prices. Other airlines also were expected to match the fares.

Tom Parsons, editor of Best Fares Discount Travel Magazine, said he could not remember the last time fares were this low.

The $75 one-way fares can be purchased through July 23 for travel from Aug. 19 to Oct. 31 on any of Southwest's published nonstop routes nationwide.

LOVE

BERLIN (AP) – The booming beat of techno music thundered through the center of Berlin on Saturday as hundreds of thousands of young people converged for the eighth annual "Love Parade."

Police estimated the crowd at 400,000 to 500,000, while organizers said 600,000 were dancing in the streets between Ernst Reuter Platz and the Brandenburg Gate.

The Love Parade tradition started in 1989 with about 150 people dancing behind a Volks-wagen van under the motto "Peace, Happiness and Pancakes." It has grown to become the world's biggest party for fans of electronic dance music known as techno.

Some 40 trucks with giant loudspeakers provided the beat for this year's parade, which was carried live by MTV Europe for the first time. People came from as far away as Japan and Australia for the party, which adopted "We are one family" as this year's motto.

RAPPER

BIRMINGHAM, Ala. (AP) – Christopher Martin, half of the rap duo "Kid 'N Play," says he's bounced back from the pitfalls of quick celebrity.

Martin, who shot to stardom as rapper "Play," says he wasn't prepared to handle fame. He had women, custom-made cars, a chain of barbershops and a clothing line.

Martin squandered his riches and had a playboy attitude. He became so depressed he considered suicide.

EXERCISE: HEADLINE WRITING AND STORY EDITING
Edit this story and write a headline as specified by your instructor.

SOCCER

The game had been tied at 1 for more than 20 minutes, and it was beginning to look like overtime was imminent for the Rock Bridge-Hickman soccer game Tuesday.

That was, until Kate Thornburg stepped up to take a direct kick just outside and to the right of the penalty box. The Kewpies formed a four-person wall, but it did no good. Thornburg lofted the ball over keeper Kate Kelly's outstretched arms, just under the crossbar and into the net for the tie-breaking goal.

The Bruins won 2-1.

It was Thornburg's first goal of her high school career.

"I was really excited," the freshman said. "I couldn't breathe for a second. But it was good. I'm glad it was this game.

"The only thing I could say, truthfully, is that I didn't even know I had to kick it. Coach just said, 'Kate, take your time,' so I realized I was supposed to kick it. Actually, it was supposed to go over to the people on the other side, but I'm glad it went in."

It was a little more special to her to score against a crosstown rival.

Since many of the players on the two teams are friends, having played on youth teams or recreation teams together, the rivalry does not carry on beyond the field. But once the whistle blows, all friendships are on hold.

"Once we are on the field," Hickman's Dee Lamphear said, "it is total concentration."

Another aspect that made this year's game more intense was the success of both teams. Rock Bridge's record is 10-3-1, and Hickman's record is 9-2.

"No matter what the record is, it is always a good game," Kewpies forward Tammy Thomas said.

A teammate, Kate David, said, "We are really, really, even, if you compare our teams."

"It was anybody's game," Rock Bridge's Jenna McAllister said.

"I thought both teams played well, and that's why I think districts will be so exciting because it will be anybody's game. Of course, coming into tonight we all knew it was anybody's game," she said.

Hickman Coach Sandy Paulsen said Tuesday's game was typical of Hickman and Rock Bridge.

"The emotions in this game are always higher," Paulsen said. "It always is when you play Rock Bridge. (Our players) get pumped up for it, and I keep telling them it is just another game and that we have got to use it to prepare us for the next time."

EXERCISE: HEADLINE WRITING AND STORY EDITING
Edit this story and write a headline as specified by your instructor.

ASHLAND

ASHLAND — Contenders for seats on the City Council, school board and fire protection district will face off at a   candidates forum at 7 p.m. Thursday in the Southern Springfield County High School gym.

Water district issues and continued citywide growth top the list of concerns that City Council candidates are expected to address. The city applied for a $300,000 matching block grant from the state last month to improve the water system and expects the outcome this summer.

"The water system is a definite concern," said Kevin Dooley, veterinarian and Chamber of Commerce member. "They're talking about putting a new water tower on the west side of town, but it's not going to be bigger than the last one. I'd like to hear if they'll put in a taller one to get more water pressure."

Second Ward Alderwoman Linda Ricks said the city is "struggling right now to make the best of how to handle the water grant, if we get it or not, and to find some money for the streets." New council members also will face the needs of a rapidly growing community.

"Three full-time police officers are fine right now, but we're growing so fast," she said. "We're not such a sleepy little town anymore."

Prospective school board members are expected to address budget problems, their interpretation of a board member's role and a new middle school concept.

In the past, the board has been forced to cut sports programs and forego teachers' salary increases. The most important question candidates probably will face is "what they feel their role is in the running of the school," said elementary school Principal Dave Decker, who has been with the district for 14 years. "And, of course, the new middle-school concept."

The board wants to formulate long-range plans for a middle school that will group students in the sixth, seventh and eigth grades in one building, instead of the seventh-, eighth- and ninth-grade junior high. The concept also might involve team teaching and some aspects of outcome-based education. "It's a different approach as far as teaching and classes go," board member Lenard Lenger said.

No prominent issues face the Fire Protection District for this election.

The Ashland Area Chamber of Commerce is sponsoring the forum. Candidates will field questions from the media and public and will make individual statements. The election will be held Tuesday.

EXERCISE: HEADLINE WRITING AND STORY EDITING
Edit this story and write a headline as specified by your instructor.

BUDGET

ASHLAND — After more than a month of negotiations, the City Council quietly approved Ashland's budget for the 2003-04 fiscal year.

The council gave the budget a unanimous nod last week at its first regular meeting since the April 6 election.

However, First Ward Alderman Billy Joe Sapp expressed concern about the amount of money designated for water improvements. The city is awaiting word on a matching block grant from the state to enlarge water lines and build a new water tower.

"The only thing that bothers me is if we don't get our grant, our water project will come into short funding," Sapp said.

Mayor Sue Turner said the project is a high priority for Ashland and the city will consider using more money from the $700,000 bond issue that was passed last November. The city originally had planned to spend $300,000 on the water project, but Turner said the council has the option of spending more if the grant is refused.

In other action:

•The council certified the results of the April 6 election, and Sapp and Second Ward Alderman Morris Stokes were sworn in. The council reappointed Alderman Dale Helms as mayor pro tem.

•Turner presented former Second Ward Alderwoman Linda Ricks a certificate of appreciation.

•The council decided to replace an old street light at College and Ash streets with one containing a brighter bulb after residents at 208 and 210 N. College St. complained it was too dark. An additional light will be placed in front of 208 N. College St. if the new light does not brighten the area.

•The council granted business licenses to And Toys Again and More at 207 West Broadway and Doug's Tobacco at 509 S. Henry Clay Blvd.

•Helms reported that residents have complained about speeding cars on Broadway from the Phillips 66 station to the highway ramp. The council will ask police to increase patrols in the area.

EXERCISE: HEADLINE WRITING AND STORY EDITING
Edit this story and write a headline as specified by your instructor.

BOONVILLE — The last time riverboats had their heyday in this town was the turn of the last century, when showboats full of party goers, musicians and actors drifted between Boonville's two bridges.

Actually, the mid-19th century marked the last time these boats dominated in the town's affairs. It marked the last time people actually used the steamer to chase the American dream, the dream of starting a new life, the dream of economic prosperity.

In this era, the steamboat pilot was "King of the River." Aided by massive, spark-shooting smokestacks and churning, splashing side wheels, this hero negotiated the unruly Missouri, landing scores of settlers in Cooper and Howard counties. His boats bore names like "The Independence" and "Western Engineer."

Now, with city voters' recent approval of riverboat gambling, the new Missouri River pilots are coming to town, banking on making big money.

But the new pilots won't be transporting Easterners eager to blaze down the Santa Fe trail. Instead, boats will bring dice-throwers, wheel-spinners and card sharks eager for some action and a fast buck.

"Historically, Boonville took advantage of the river. It was our original economic stimulus," said Steve Goehl, Boonville's city administrator, who has spearheaded the gaming plan since this summer. "Then the railroads came and dominated transportation for a while. Then, there was the Interstate. What we're trying to do is recapture the riverfront."

In last week's election, citizens agreed firmly, if not wholeheartedly, with Goehl's vision. Just under 59 percent of voters approved the idea of local gaming excursions on riverboats. In the two waterfront districts, flood-damaged Wards One and Two, voters showed strong agreement, with support of 64 percent and 57 percent, respectively.

Even before the Great Flood of '93 manhandled the city's waterfront, residents wanted to rebuild the sad riverside. In a November 1992 vote on statewide riverboat gambling, 63 percent of Boonville voters approved. In Cooper County, 71 percent approved. This year's vote allowed citizens to approve gambling in individual cities.

Now, the city's Industrial Development Authority — an independent panel of local business leaders — will recommend who gets the Boonville steamboat pilot's cap. Five organizations, one of whom is a group of anonymous investors from Columbia, are competing for the city's approval.

The City Council, advised by the industrial authority, will make the final decision on the choice developer. The last obstacle for that developer will be getting a license from the newly created Missouri Gaming Commission.

The commission has 207 pages of rules and regulations, plus state statutes, concerning riverboat gambling. It's up to commissioners' discretion whether Boonville's plan gets approved, said Sgt. Kenneth Hoelker, investigator with the commission in St. Louis.

"Anyone in the state can apply. The state is open to any legitimate game of chance," he said.

When the developer returns with the license, the city will "guide" plans for riverfront development, preserving the area's historical tone, making sure the Water Street area comes first and foremost.

"The City has significant interest in access and development of an area between the Missouri River Highway Bridge west to the Railroad Crossing Bridge," according to the city's gaming document. "The City would entertain the possibility of development in another location .|.|. however, the above mentioned site remains the city's top priority."

All costs — from construction to boat maintenance to security against gambling-related crime — will fall on the developer. City officials put up $5,000 for last week's election, and that's all they'll spend on riverboat gambling.

"We intend to stick to our promise," Goehl said. "There has been no further allocation. We'd have to amend our budget, and I'd advise the City Council against it."

What will the city get in return? Officials estimate that 150 to 200 new private-sector jobs could be created. No extra city employees would be needed. Finally, the city treasury could collect about $1 million in additional tax revenue.

That revenue will come from two sources: The city will collect a $1 fee from every passenger who enters the boat. Also, Boonville will get 2 percent of the boat's adjusted gross revenue.

Along with taxes, city officials will have high standards and high expectations for whoever opens up a local gambling operation, Goehl said.

"We intentionally set these standards high to make sure we have the best overall development," he said. "We set them high to protect the city."

Many believe violence, namely from organized crime, will follow gambling into town. These citizens, who voted "no" in last week's election, make it seem like Boonville is poised to take a moral dive back to the shoot-'em-up frontier days, only with modern-day bad guys.

But Mayor Bernard Kempf does not share these doubts — not at a time when Boonville can regain its historical identity, as well as its prosperity, from a river that has brought only wrack and ruin lately.

"I've never had doubts," Kempf said. "I've always been for development, for things to happen. That's what this is."

9

Using Photos, Graphics and Type

Student Name _____ Course _____ Date_____

QUIZ: USING PHOTOS, GRAPHICS AND TYPE
Circle T for true or F for false.

T F   1. Graphic appeal is essential to all media except radio.

T F   2. Only about 30 percent of readers enter pages through large photos, artwork or display type.

T F   3. Headlines are more likely to be read when photos are nearby.

T F   4. Good publications treat photos and graphics as the equivalent of stories.

T F   5. Visual literacy is not important for word editors as long as photo editors have it.

T F   6. Photographers must be treated as important members of the staff.

T F   7. Photo selection is important.

T F   8. Cropping skills are important for editors at the newspaper design desk.

T F   9. Most photos are handled electronically, although a few publications still use film and contact prints.

T F   10. Size contrast is important in multiple-picture packages.

T F   11. Retouching is permitted only for correcting minor imperfections in photos.

T F   12. Digital photography is dominant at publications today.

T F   13. Photos never lie.

T F   14. Some photographers have won Pulitzer Prizes.

T F   15. Captions should have specifics, not generalities.

T F   16. Photo captions should state the obvious.

T F   17. Maps help readers locate things.

T F   18. Pie charts show how parts of the whole are divided.

T F   19. Process drawings help readers visualize detailed plans or progressive action.

T F   20. Sans-serif type is more difficult to read than serifed type when sized as body type.

PROBLEMS: USING PHOTOS AND GRAPHICS IN PRINT

1. Find an example of a picture you believe your newspaper should not have used. On what is your opinion based? Defend your position.

2. You are working as the news editor of a newspaper in Williamsburg, Va. You must decide whether to publish the fire tragedy pictures shown in the textbook (Figures 11-7A and 11-7B). What is your decision? Defend your position.

3. As news editor of the Williamsburg paper, once again you are confronted with a decision about whether to publish pictures of a tragedy. This time the picture shows the mangled body of a local woman killed in a traffic accident. She was well-known in the community for her civic work. Would you publish the picture? Why or why not?

4. The wire services have transmitted a picture of the vice president making an obscene gesture to hecklers during a speech. Should you publish the picture? Why or why not?

PROBLEMS: AN INTRODUCTION TO USING TYPE

1. Your publisher has asked you to suggest a typeface to be used for headlines. Her instructions are to select a face that reflects the history or your newspaper as an old, reliable publication. Suggest three typefaces and defend your choices.

2. Inspect the body type of two newspapers readily available to you. Identify the typefaces and tell which one you believe is more legible. Explain your position.

3. Find an example of poor spacing in a newspaper. Explain what you would have done to eliminate the problem.

4. You are the news editor of your local newspaper, which is planning to install a pagination system. The computer vendor has asked you to list specifications for spacing within the newspaper. List all the important spacing standards, such as space between columns, horizontal space between stories, and so forth.

EXERCISE: CAPTION WRITING
Write a photo caption for the photo on the reverse side as specified by your instructor.

Photo Caption

Photographer:

Adrianna Vaz

Date:

May 12

Department:

News

Ordered by:

Martinez

SLUG: FAIR

Roger DeGregorio, 10, of Hallsville gives his hog a firm
yank by the tail in an attempt to make the hog pay attention.
Roger is exhibiting the hog, whose name is "Junior," at
the Boone County Fair. The fair ends Friday at the Boone
County Fair Grounds.

Student Name _____ Course _____ Date_____

EXERCISE: CAPTION WRITING
Write a photo caption for the photo on the reverse side as specified by your instructor.

Photo Caption

Photographer:

Taylor Burkett

Date:

Aug. 13

Department:

News

Ordered by:

Langton

SLUG: WRECK

Paramedics assist Dennis Rodriguez after removing him from his wrecked car at Broadway and College Street. Rodriguez was taken to University hospital, where he was in serious condition today with head injuries. Police have not yet determined the cause of the mishap.

EXERCISE: CAPTION WRITING
Write a photo caption for the photo on the reverse side as specified by your instructor.

Photo Caption

Photographer:

Wanda Reynolds

Date:

Oct.11

Department:

News

Ordered by:

Wu

SLUG: PLANE

Richard Anderson of Dubuque, Iowa managed to survive the crash of his private jet plane on Tuesday. "I'm lucky to be alive," he said, after the plane suddenly lost power and landed in a field seven miles northeast of Springfield. The land is owned by farmer Rondell Utterback.

EXERCISE: CAPTION WRITING
Write a photo caption for the photo on the reverse side as specified by your instructor.

Photo Caption

Photographer:

Indira Wekli

Date:

June 10

Department:

News

Ordered by:

Barber

SLUG: ROLLED

A truck driven by Elbert McDill of Boulder, CO, overturned in the median of Interstate 70 Sunday just east of Springfield. McDill said he swerved to avoid a car stopped in the passing lane and lost control. The truck overturned and was heavily damaged. McDill, who was alone in the truck, was not hurt. The wreck slowed traffic for 45 minutes as onlookers gawked.

EXERCISE: HANDLING MULTIPLE-PHOTO PACKAGES
Determine how you would use these photos as specified by your instructor.

Photo Caption

Photographer:

Adrianna Vaz

Date:

April 11

Department:

News

Ordered by:

Wu

SLUG: FIRE

Deborah Blake, left, a paramedic, and John Rackers, a fireman, lead Linda Longley out of her burning house at 311 Williams Street at 3:15 p.m. Tuesday. Am unidentified fireman tried to extinguish the fire in the attic by going through he roof while another fireman, Richard Anderson, was briefly overcome by smoke and sought a bit of relief by sitting on the back of his fire truck. Cause and extent of damage are unknown..

213

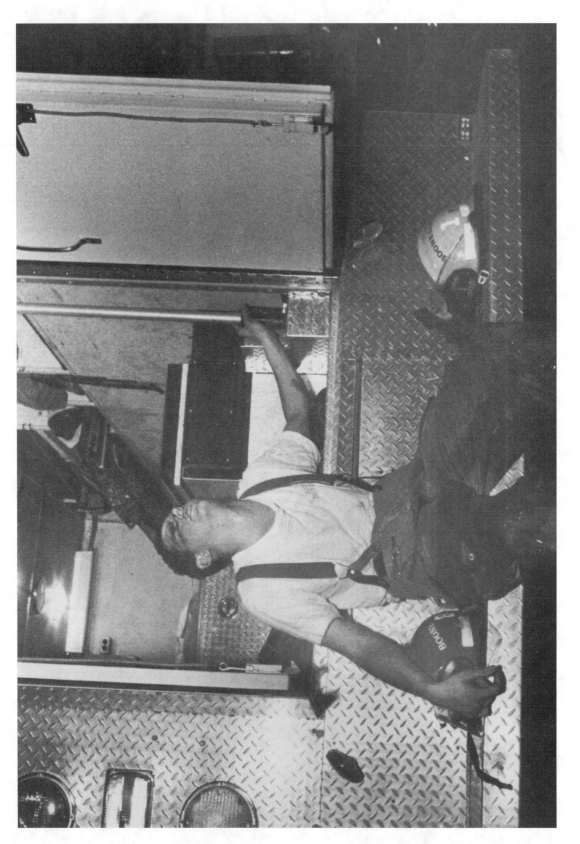

10

Editing Newspapers

Student Name _____ Course _____ Date_____

PROBLEMS: AN INTRODUCTION TO NEWSPAPER LAYOUT AND DESIGN

1. Describe, in your own words, the purposes of newspaper design.

2. Take a front page from your local newspaper and describe how the layout artist or designer has used the principles of artistic design.

3. Using copies of three newspapers to which you have access, describe the design concepts involved. Tell whether you consider them to be traditional or contemporary. Why?

4. Take a copy of a page that you consider to be poorly designed. Rework the page using the same elements.

Student Name _____ Course _____ Date_____

EXERCISE: EDITING NEWSPAPERS

Design a page using the material listed here. Your ad dummy is on the reverse side. Your instructor will provide further instructions.

Editor's Copy Log

Name _____ Date_____ Desk _____

Story Slug	Time Received	Time Moved	Head Size	Length
RIDGEWAY	1:15	1:35	HTK	12"
RIDGEWAY CUT			3 col X 6"	
MILLER	1:20	2:00	HTK	7"
LONESTAR	1:25	2:00	HTK	7½"
REINDEER	1:30	2:05	HTK	3"
FULLER	1:35	2:10	HTK	6"

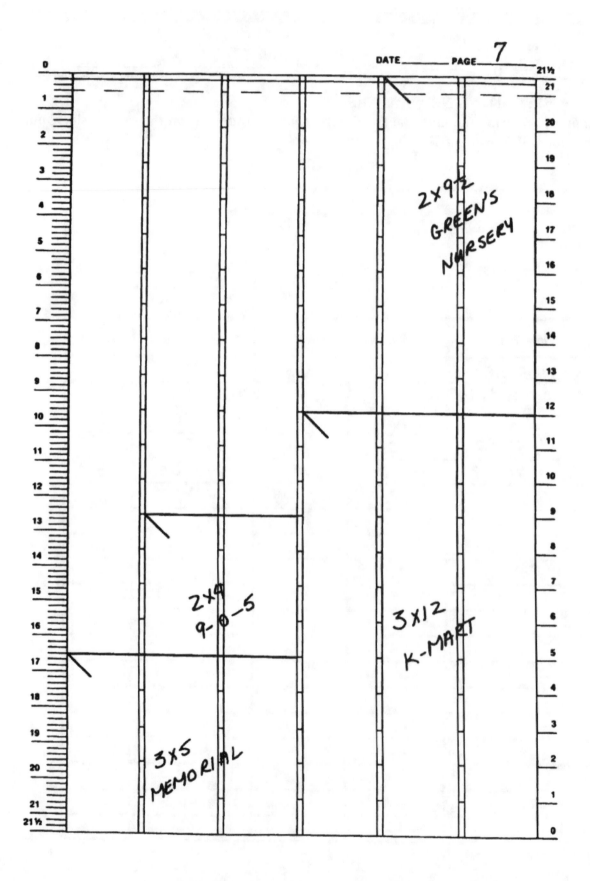

EXERCISE: EDITING NEWSPAPERS

Design a page using the material listed here. Your ad dummy is on the reverse side. Your instructor will provide further instructions.

Editor's Copy Log

Name _____ Date_____ Desk _____

Story Slug	Time Received	Time Moved	Head Size	Length
SCHMIDT	4:20	4:35	HTK	6"
ISRAEL	4:30	4:50	HTK	8"
ISRAEL PIC			3 COL X 4"	
LEBANON	4:35	4:50		6"
VATICAN	4:35	4:55	HTK	12"
AFRICA	4:40	5:00	HTK	8"
MEXICO	4:40	5:05	HTK	5"
ULSTER	4:45	5:05	HTK	10"
MILLER	4:45	5:00	HTK	$2\frac{1}{2}$"

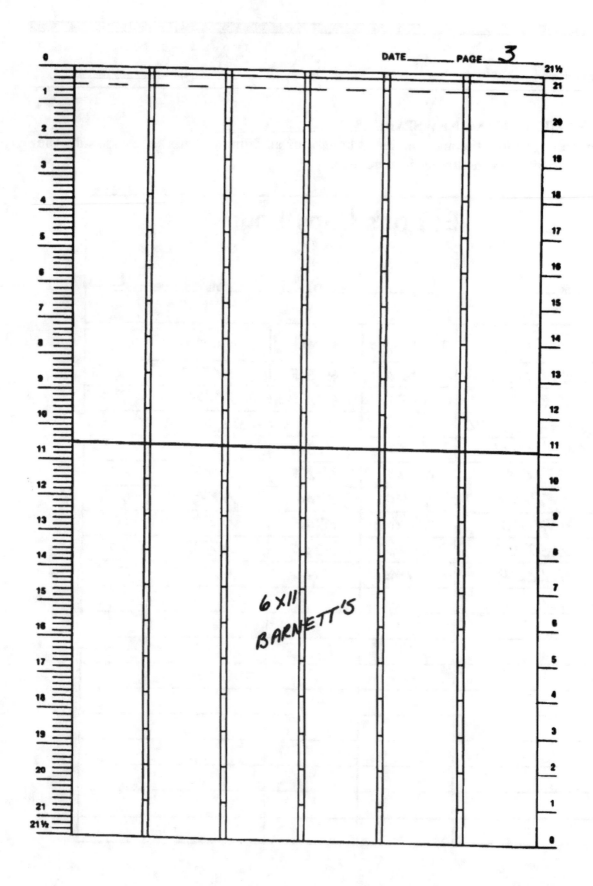

DATE_____ PAGE __3__

6 X 11
BARNETT'S

EXERCISE: EDITING NEWSPAPERS
Design a page using the material listed here. Your ad dummy is on the reverse side. Your instructor will provide further instructions.

Editor's Copy Log

Name _____ Date_____ Desk _____

Story Slug	Time Received	Time Moved	Head Size	Length
ATLANTA	2:05	2:30	HTK	12"
BANK	2:05	2:35	HTK	8"
MUSIC	2:08	2:40	HTK	9"
SCHOOL	2:10	2:40	HTK	8"
SCHOOL PIC			2 col X 4"	
GRAVE	2:15	2:45		5"
DONOR	2:20	2:50	HTK	12"

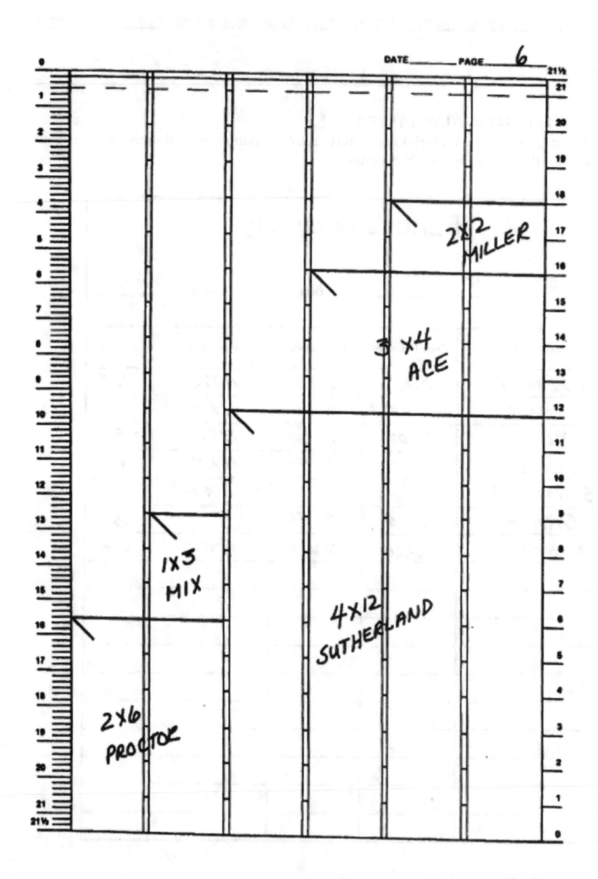

DATE _____ PAGE ____ 6 ____

2X2 MILLER

3 X4 ACE

4X12 SUTHERLAND

1X3 MIX

2X6 PROCTOR

Student Name _____ Course _____ Date_____

EXERCISE: EDITING NEWSPAPERS
Design a page using the material listed here. Your ad dummy is on the reverse side. Your instructor will provide further instructions.

Editor's Copy Log

Name _____ Date_____ Desk _____

Story Slug	Time Received	Time Moved	Head Size	Length
TRAIN PIC	5:00		3 col x 5"	CUTLINE ONLY
MILLER	5:15	5:45	HTK	10"
WILTON	5:20	5:55	HTK	12"
DENTON	5:25	6:00	HTK	8"
ROUND UP	5:30	6:10	HTK	15"
PRESIDENT	5:40	6:20	HTK	20"
AIM PIC	5:45		4 col X 5"	CUTLINE ONLY

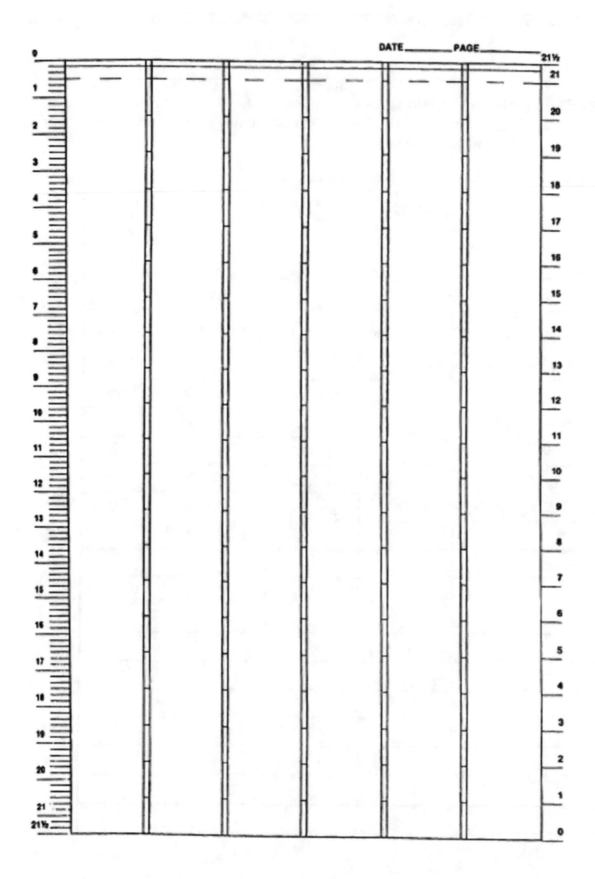

DATE_____ PAGE_____

Copyright © 2009 Pearson Education, Inc. Publishing as Allyn & Bacon.

EXERCISE: EDITING NEWSPAPERS
Design a page using the material listed here. Your ad dummy is on the reverse side. Your instructor will provide further instructions.

Editor's Copy Log

Name _____ Date _____ Desk _____

Story Slug	Time Received	Time Moved	Head Size	Length
BUDGET	9:25	9:50	HTK	12"
BUDGET CHARTS (2)	2 COL X 4 (both)			
MAYOR	9:40	10:25	HTK	9"
MIDEAST	9:50	10:35	HTK	15"
WEATHER CUT	(lines only)		3 COL X 6"	
TRIP	10:10	10:43	HTK	12"
TRIP CUT			1 COL X 3"	
SENATE	10:20	11:00	HTK	9"
THINK	10:25	11:10	HTK	6"

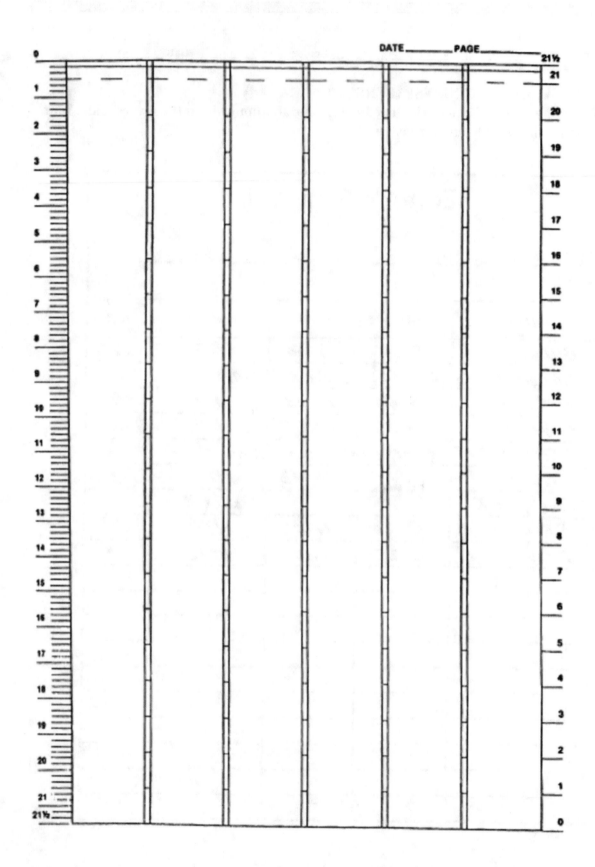

DATE_____ PAGE_____

228

11

Editing Magazines and Newsletters

Student Name _____ Course _____ Date_____

QUIZ: OVERVIEW
Circle T for true or F for false.

T F 1. Surprisingly, magazine jobs tend to pay less than comparable newspaper ones.

T F 2. Staff positions at magazines tend to be editorial ones because many magazines use free-lance writers for much of their content.

T F 3. The word magazine comes from the Arabic through the French. It means a storehouse, as of ammunition.

T F 4. Magazines first probably developed in 17th-century France from bookseller catalogs.

T F 5. There are perhaps as many as 2,000 consumer magazines in the United States and 12,000 specialty magazines – but by the time you add in PR magazines, newsletters, and industry and association publications, there are perhaps 50,000 magazines in the United States.

T F 6. Fewer than 20 percent of the 1,000 or so magazines started each year are still publishing two years later.

T F 7. The average American household subscribes only to one magazine.

T F 8. No magazine has as much circulation as USA Today.

T F 9. Good sources for the names and addresses of magazines are *Writer's Market, Bowker's Working Press of the Nation* and the *Gale Directory of Publications*.

T F 10. Trade publications, like trade books, are aimed at the general consumer audience.

T F 11. The fastest-growing category of all print publications, not counting the Internet, is the newsletter.

T F 12. If you want to work for a consumer magazine, two job hints include going to work first for a smaller publication, such as a corporate or trade or association one, and having an interest in copy editing.

T F 13. The managing editor is the person who most guides the magazine along a certain vision.

T F 14. "Senior editor" is another name for "section editor."

T F 15. Magazines should be redesigned whenever there's a change in ownership or editor to signal the all-new direction.

T F 16. Magazines are less restricted in design than are newspapers.

T F 17. It's usually not a good idea to use cover lines to sell regular departments.

T F 18. A good publication design is one that calls attention to itself.

T F 19. Newsletters could be considered one of the earliest forms of written journalism.

T F 20. Quoting sources like *The New York Times* is a good way for a newsletter to establish credibility.

Student Name _____ Course _____ Date_____

PROBLEMS: MAGAZINES

1. What companies, associations, organizations, government agencies, or so on that are in your area publish magazines or newsletters for employees, members, customers, an industry, etc.? Find one that interests you, get a copy of its publication, then look into the possibility of an internship.

2. Pick a magazine you enjoy reading and look in the front to see where it's published and by what company. Then, using the Web, look into what other magazines that company publishes. Get a copy of some of the other magazines that company owns, then compare them. Are they on similar topics? Do they look alike? How similar is the style of writing?

Student Name _____ Course _____ Date_____

PROBLEM: NEWSLETTER BUSINESS PLAN
In two double-spaced pages, write a proposal for a newsletter you could start that you think might be successful.

Use the following questions as suggestions for information to include:

- Who is the target audience, and what do they have in common?

- What would you call it? What would the design be like?   How many pages would it be per issue?

- How would you drum up publicity among potential readers that the newsletter was being published? How would you market it?

- What is the purpose of the newsletter?

- What competition would it face, and how would your newsletter find a niche of its own?

- How often would it be published? Would it be published in hard copy and mailed or be published on the Internet through a Web site or by e-mail?

- What would it cost you to produce it? For what price, if any, would it be sold?

- What resources do you have that you could use to produce it? What resources would you need to get? How would you get them?

- Would you offer related products for sale through your own mail-order store? If so, what kinds of products?

12

Editing
for the Web

Student Name _____ Course _____ Date_____

QUIZ: EDITING FOR THE WEB
Circle T for true or F for false.

T F   1. Tradtional media often are viewed as "preachy and arrogant."

T F   2. The Web often challenges established norms of journalistic ethics.

T F   3. Editors can make web content easier to read by using layers and links.

T F   4. The online journalist is a converged journalist.

T F   5. Journalists may lift information from web sites without verification.

T F   6. The address of a site can give tips about the veracity of information.

T F   7. MSNBC is a public information utility.

T F   8. The Internet has become the most dominant of the online services.

T F   9. CD-ROMs can be a publishing medium.

T F   10. Commercial database services provide access to hundreds of newspaper and magazine libraries and are invaluable to journalists.

T F   11. Journalists can lift any material from commercial database services for reuse.

T F   12. Government databases cannot be trusted for information.

T F   13. Special interest groups publish databases, and the material on them is often free. Journalists can rest assured that information on those services is accurate.

T F   14. Online editors are multimedia journalists.

T F   15. An accomplished editor can easily become an accomplished graphics artist thanks to computers.

T F   16. The World Wide Web transformed use of the Internet, which had been around for years.

T F   17. URL stands for United Research Laboratories.

T F   18. Web designers should put the best information at the top of the page so users don't have to scroll down.

T F   19. Web designers are free to use any background color.

T F   20. High-speed connections to homes are essential for the web to reach its full potential.

PROBLEMS: WEB EDITING

1. Compare the coverage of a news event on television with what you can find on the Internet. Which is more comprehensive? Why?

2. Discuss the relationship of newspapers, television and the new media. List the ways in which they complement each other as well as compete.

3. Read a news story on America Online, MSNBC or the BBC Web site. Compare and contrast the coverage of that story to what appears in your local newspaper the next day. In what ways do the accounts differ?

4. Find 10 news sources on the World Wide Web that you consider to be of high quality. List their URLs.

13

Editing
for the Broadcast Media

CHAPTER 13 OVERVIEW
Circle T for true or F for false.

T F   1. Most of the techniques for editing print apply as well to editing broadcast copy.

T F   2. The top news executive at a broadcast station is normally called the "executive producer."

T F   3. Broadcast copy is normally double-spaced.

T F   4. Broadcast copy on a TelePrompTer or hard-copy script typically has only about four words a line.

T F   5. Broadcast copy should include pronunciation guides for any unusual names.

T F   6. Most abbreviations are not acceptable in broadcast copy, but those that are use hyphens instead of periods.

T F   7. Dashes or ellipses are often used in place of a comma to show the newsletter when to pause and breathe.

T F   8. Contractions are not acceptable in broadcast copy.

T F   9. Direct quotations are seldom used in copy read by a broadcaster.

T F 10. The attribution should come before a quotation in broadcast copy.

T F 11. Instead of writing that a suspect was "50 to 60 years old," in broadcast you should write he was "between 50 and 60 years old."

T F 12. Fractions, decimals, one-digit numbers and numbers more than 999 are written out in broadcast style.

T F 13. Any titles should normally precede a person's name.

T F 14. Datelines should be converted to introductions or moved elsewhere in the lead.

T F 15. Broadcasters seldom say "today," because most things reported on happened today.

T F 16. Television writing should be done in the past and past-perfect tenses.

T F 17. All broadcast copy should include the date, time block, story slug, writer's name or initials, story source and indication of whether the story has a companion audio or video segment.

T F 18. Cue lines should be provided – usually marked in red – where each recorded segment is to be inserted.

T F 19. Recorded segments in stories should be grouped as closely together as possible.

T F 20. News editing requires more time for television than radio.

Student Name _____ Course _____ Date_____

EXERCISE: BROADCAST EDITING
Edit this story for broadcast as directed by your instructor.

DEATHROW

A federal appeals court on Monday night denied a request for a stay by death row inmate Lloyd Rusk, clearing the way for his scheduled execution early Friday.

Rusk, 32, formerly of Springfield, is to die by lethal injection at 12:01 a.m. Friday for his role in the murder of a fellow inmate, Arthur "Stump" Smith, in the high-security lockdown wing of the old State Penitentiary in Smithton. The murder occurred Feb. 3, 1994. He is on death row at the Oregondale Correctional Center, about 60 miles south of Springfield.

A three-judge panel of the 8th U.S. Circuit Court of Appeals voted 2-1 to deny the appeal and vacate the stay.

In the appeal, Rusk's attorney presented several affidavits and statements, mostly from present or former prisoners, that Rusk wasn't present at the scene of the murder. A videotape offered at his trial showing him in the dining room near the time of the murder also was reintroduced.

EXERCISE: BROADCAST EDITING
Edit this story for broadcast as directed by your instructor.

CRACK

Lavonda Beck was inconsolable Thursday when she testified that Norbert A. Sansome killed Jeff Barber over a crack deal.

Sansome, 23, is charged with second-degree murder and armed criminal action. He is being held at the Springfield County Jail on a $500,000 bond.

Beck, 28, of Springfield said during a preliminary hearing in Springfield County Circuit Court, that Sansome killed Barber, 20, with a single gunshot. Boone County Circuit Judge Jodie Asel bound the case for trial.

The incident began the morning of Jan. 25, when Barber and Beck drove to 815 Grand Ave. to buy crack. Beck said Barber parked and walked to the crack house. Barber bought the drug and returned to the car, but Sansome followed him and asked him to get out, she said.

``Give me the money or the dope," she said Sasome told Barber. Beck said Barber begged for his life, but Sansome shot him while they were arguing.

Although shot, Barber got into the car and drove away with Beck. Two blocks later, his car hit a parked car, causing both cars to hit a house. Beck was unhurt. Barber died hours that Norbert A. Sansome killed Jeff Barber over a crack deal.

Sansome, 23, is charged with second-degree murder and armed criminal action. He is being held at the Springfield County Jail on a $500,000 bond.

EXERCISE: BROADCAST EDITING
Edit this story for broadcast as directed by your instructor.

TAILLIGHT

A broken taillight led to the arrest of a Chicago man in Springfield Monday on suspicion of felony tampering in connection with a car stolen earlier that day. Police are still trying to determine why he had a suitcase in the car containing $15,000.

On a routine patrol, police officers noticed the car with a defective taillight at Washington Avenue and Pecan Street, ran the license plate and found the car was stolen, said Capt. Mick Covington of the Springfield Police Department.

On a routine patrol, police officers pulled the car over and arrested the driver, Michael D. Bellinghausen. He faces charges of tampering and a warrant for failing to appear in court at an earlier date. He also faces charges of driving with a suspended license.

The Circuit Clerk's Office said Bellinghausen has not posted his $20,248 bond and remains in the Springfield County Jail.

Just why the $15,000 was in the car remains a mystery. Police said the cash was in a briefcase in the back seat. Bellinghausen refused to tell where it came from but insisted it was his.

14

Editing in Other Fields

Student Name _____ Course _____ Date_____

QUIZ: OVERVIEW
Circle T for true or F for false.

T F   1. Public relations and advertising are not media but adjuncts to it.

T F   2. About half of news stories originate from a press release.

T F   3. Advertising is more covert than public relations.

T F   4. Public relations, like advertising, is regulated by the government.

T F   5. Public relations messages only become news if a journalist agrees they're newsworthy.

T F   6. One place advertising students get their first job is working in advertising departments of media outlets.

T F   7. Public relations and advertising jobs tend to pay more than comparable media jobs.

T F   8. Historically, women have not risen as fast in public relations and advertising as they have in reporting and editing jobs.

T F   9. The No. 1 trait people hiring for public relations positions look for is good writing skills.

T F 10. Press releases should be written like advertisements for the person, cause or event being promoted.

T F 11. The book-publishing industry has not been doing as well since the rise of the popularity of television.

T F 12. Most books published are nonfiction.

T F 13. The two main ways to get a job in the book-publishing industry in New York are to start at a university or specialty press, or to attend a publishing institute such as the one at Columbia University.

T F 14. The best magazines to follow to learn about the book-publishing industry include *Publishers Weekly, Retail Bookseller* and the *New York Review of Books.*

T F 15. Entry-level jobs in book publishing are highly competitive partly because the pay is so good compared to what journalists typically make.

T F 16. Turnover is rapid in book publishing, similar to broadcast.

T F 17. Copy editing, book design and indexing are often done by free-lancers in the book-publishing business.

T F 18. Book publishers no longer typically work with hard-copy manuscripts but solely with computer files.

T F 19. A book typically doesn't appear in print until about 18 months after the original signing.

T F 20. *The Chicago Manual of Style* is a common stylebook used in the book world.

Student Name _____ Course _____ Date_____

PROBLEMS: EDITING ADVERTISING

1. Find a print advertisement in which you consider the relationship between the photo and the text to be lacking. Explain why you think this is so.

2. Clip six ads from a magazine, three that you consider to be good ones and three you do not like. Tell why you like or dislike each one.

Student Name _____ Course _____ Date_____

PROBLEMS: PUBLIC RELATIONS

1. Ask two people who work professionally in public relations what role writing and editing skills play on their job. Also, ask if they were hiring someone right out of college whether they would prefer someone with a degree in public relations or in journalism.

2. Call a local newspaper and ask the city editor about how many press releases the paper receives a week and how many are actually published in some form. Also, ask what is typically done to the releases that are used in order to make them publishable. What advice would the editor give to people hoping to get their press releases published?

PROBLEMS: BOOK PUBLISHING

1. Find out what university and specialty presses there are near you, and using the Web, look into them. What kinds of books to they publish? If you wanted to start on a career in book publishing, which ones would be of most interest to you as a place to get an internship or first job? Use this information to write a letter applying for an internship or job.

2. Compare the current New York Times Best Sellers list with one from the same time last year. Can you note any patterns within each list or between the two lists that shed light on what kinds of books or subjects are the most popular?

15

The Editor As Coach

Student Name _____ Course _____ Date_____

QUIZ: THE EDITOR AS COACH
Circle T for true or F for false.

T F 1. The editing of stories at good publications is a repetitive process.

T F 2. A story may be edited a dozen times at top publications.

T F 3. Reporters should take criticism of their writing as a personal affront.

T F 4. The assigning editor helps the reporter plot the story line.

T F 5. The reporting process is totally unlike the scientific investigation process.

T F 6. The reporter and assigning editor often review the story together.

T F 7. Clark and Fry argue that the writing process works best when the reporter and editors share control of a story.

T F 8. Some stories need no editing, according to Clark and Fry.

T F 9. Fixing takes over when there is no time for coaching.

T F 10. Creative tension is a productive process that should be used in all newsrooms.

T F 11. Producing editors transform the work of the assigning editor and reporter into a finished product.

T F 12. It's impossible for a reporter to get "too close" to a story.

T F 13. Stories with internal inconsistencies are rare.

T F 14. Copy editors often get the last crack at a story before it is published.

T F 15. Good editors learn by emulating the best editors they encounter.

T F 16. Supervising editors often do not provide enough feedback for junior editors to improve their skills.

T F 17. If you don't like how your editors deal with you, complain loudly.

T F 18. Editors typically have no ethical problems.

16

The Editor As Manager and Leader

Student Name _____ Course _____ Date_____

QUIZ: THE EDITOR AS MANAGER AND LEADER
Circle T for true or F for false.

T F   1. Editors are managers, and the best ones are leaders.

T F   2. Gentry's Law is that editors are prime examples of the Peter Principle.

T F   3. Newspaper managers are known for their great management skills.

T F   4. Managing and leading are the same thing with different names.

T F   5. Performance is based on ability, motivation and role perception.

T F   6. Managers hire the staff, then forget about what goes on after that.

T F   7. Staff development is a key to good management.

T F   8. Managers need to organize the staffs they manage.

T F   9. Internal communication is not necessary in media operations because communication is an essential part of the culture.

T F   10. Without planning, a news department drifts from crisis to crisis.

T F   11. Managers should not control because control is seen as harsh and counterproductive..

T F   12. Minimum standards should be established, but nothing more should be demanded..

T F   13. People enjoy being led; they tolerate being managed.

T F   14. Leaders praise accomplishment.

T F   15. Employees of those who manage may dread a visit to the boss.

T F   16. Leaders profess to know it all.

Appendix I
Symbols

Copy Editing

Indent for new paragraph

(no ¶) No paragraph (in margin)

Run in or bring copy together

Join words: week end

Insert a word or phrase

Insert a mising letter

Take out anl extra letter

Transpose words two

Transpose two letters

Make letter lower case

Capitalize columbia

Indicate italic letters

Indicate small capitals

Indicate bold face type

Abbreviate January 30

Spell out abbrev

Spell out number 9

Make figures of thirteen

Separate run together words

Join letters in a w ord

Insert period ⊙

Insert comma ⋏

Insert quotation marks ⌄⌄ ⌄⌄

Take out some word

Don't make this correction

Mark centering like this

Indent copy from both sides by using these marks

Indent copy on left

Spell name Smyth as written

or

Spell name Smyth as written

There's more story: MORE

This ends story: ⌗ 30

Do not obliterate copy; mark it out with a thin line so it can be compared with editing.

Mark in hyphen: =

Mark in dash: ⊢

a and u

ō and n̄

Proofreading

∧	Insert at this point.	√√	Space evenly.
⊥	Push down space.	◡	Close up entirely.
℘	Take out letter, letters, or words.	⊏	Move to left.
℘	Turn inverted letter.	⊐	Move to right.
(lc)	Set lowercase.	⊔	Lower letter or word.
(wf)	Wrong font letter.	⊓	Raise letter or word.
(ital)	Reset in italic type.	(out, see copy)	Words are left out.
(rom)	Reset in roman (regular) type.	∥≡	Straighten lines.
(bf)	Reset in bold face type.	¶	Start new paragraph.
⊙	Insert period.	(no ¶)	No paragraph. Run together.
⌄	Insert comma.	(tr)	Transpose letters or words.
⌄	Insert semicolon.	(?)	Query; is copy right?
⊢	Insert hyphen.	⊢⊣	Insert dash.
∨	Insert apostrophe.	☐	Indent 1 em.
∨∨	Enclose in quotation marks.	☐☐	Indent 2 ems.
≡	Replace with a capital letter.	☐☐☐	Indent 3 ems.
#	Insert space.	(stet)	Let it stand.

Appendix II
Headline Schedule

ENGLISH BOLD

Headline	Maximum	Headline	Maximum	Headline	Maximum
1-14	21	4-36	39	4-60	23 1/2
1-18	18	1-48	6 1/2	5-60	30
1-24	13	2-48	14	6-60	36
2-24	26 1/2	3-48	21	2-72	7
1-30	10 1/2	4-48	29	3-72	14 1/2
2-30	23	5-48	37	4-72	20
1-36	9	6-48	44	5-72	24 1/2
2-36	19	2-60	11 1/2	6-72	30
3-36	29	3-60	17 1/2		

Avoid using headlines not listed above. For example, 14-point English Bold would not be used across two columns.

ENGLISH LIGHT

Headline	Maximum	Headline	Maximum	Headline	Maximum
1-14	22	4-36	42	4-60	25 1/2
1-18	19	1-48	7	5-60	32
1-24	14	2-48	15	6-60	38 1/2
2-24	29	3-48	23 1/2	2-72	7 1/2
1-30	11	4-48	31 1/2	3-72	15 1/2
2-30	24	5-48	40	4-72	21 1/2
1-36	9 1/2	6-48	48	5-72	26 1/2
2-36	20 1/2	2-60	12 1/2	6-72	32
3-36	31	3-60	19		

ENGLISH EXTRABOLD

Headline	Maximum	Headline	Maximum	Headline	Maximum
1-14	16	1-30	8	1-60	4
1-18	13	1-36	6 1/2	1-72	3
1-24	10 1/2	1-48	5		

Note: To figure the maximum count for English Extrabold headlines of more than one column, multiply the maximum for one column by the number of columns.

Appendix III
Springfield
City Directory

-A-

A&B Maintenance Management Co., 512 Cherry St.

A-1 Insulation, 730 W. Sexton Rd.

Adelstein, Richard (phys, Univ. Hosp), 754 Trail Ridge

Alderson, Robert M. & Wanda (gen mgr, Boone Electric Co-op), Route 5

Alexander, Martha (dir, Univ library), 203 Edgewood

Altomani, Mark & Diana (director, Associates in Human Services), 209 Lynnwood Dr.

Aly, Thomas (emp unk), 2369 Ridge Rd.

Ambaugh, Mrs. Ardath (retired), Senior Citizens Center

American Red Cross, 1805 W. Worley St.

Amundson, Erik K. (student, University), 2012 W. Ash St., Apt. D5

Anderson, David & Lena M. (retired), 913 N. Garth Ave.

Apon, Ruth N. (sr. stenographer, University), 110 N. Glenwood Ave.

Asel, Jodie, (judge, Boone County Circuit Court), 2029 Burrwood Dr.

Ash, Kenneth (University Health Sciences Ctr), 312 Sanford Ave.

Axelhander, David (student), 206 S. Hitt St.

-B-

Ball, Barbara (animal control off.), 2045 Thilly

Ballard, Dennis (retired), 307 N. Ninth St.

Barbee, Ernest (Chief, Col. police dept), 2002 Green Meadows Rd.

Barnes, Pat (asst chief, Boone County Fire Prot. Dist.), 4202 W. Rollins Rd.

Bashor, Terry W. & Diane E. (asst. dean, University), 1317 Overhill Rd.

Bauer, Robert (prof, university), 2044 Trail Ridge

Bayte, John (United Brotherhood of Carpenters), 378 Eva Drive

Beck, LaVonda (clerk, K-mart), 233 Third St.

Beck, Raymond A. & Delilah (city mgr, City of Springfield), 201 Sappington Dr.

Bell, Dennis (mgr, University), Rt. 1 Hallsville

Belliard, Penney (waiter), Rt. 1, Centralia

Belvedere Apartrnents, 206 Hitt St.

Bevier, Patrick (fac, Rock Bridge HS), 101 First St.

Binningham, Dan (Associates in Human Services), 2002 Hinkson Ave.

Black, Robert D. & Jean C (asst city mgr), 812 Maupin Rd.

Blackwell, Doris C. (asst to pres, Boatmen's Bank), Rt. 2

Blister, Todd M. (carpenter), 134 Limerick Lane

B'nai B'rith Hillel Foundation, 909 University Ave.

Board of Education, 1818 W. Worley St.

Boehm, Randall (capt, Col. police dept), 211 Grace Ellen Dr.

Boone County Bank, 720 E Broadway

Boone Electric Co-operative, 1413 Business 63 N.

Borman, Debra (emp unk), 1901 E. Walnut St., Apt. 3

Boston, Diane (housekeeper, VA Hospital), 9 Business 63 S., Apt. 16

Bowman, Kevin (owner, Boone County Glass), 2901 Greenbriar Dr.

Bower, Rober (assoc. prof, univ.), 204 Stewart Rd.

Bradford, Betty O. (janitor), 800 Wilkes Blvd.

Braudis, Chris (supv., Red Cross), 222 S. Ninth St.

Brazos, Blaise (engr, University), 386 Tara Lane

Briggs, Mitchell (unemp), 1250 Third St.

Brill, Patricia (information specialist, Boone Hospital Ctr), 2145 Aubum Lane.

Brooks, Amanda (student), 843 Lynnwood Dr.

Brown, Nate (newspaper executive), 210 Stalcup St.

Brydon, Earl C (laborer, Walter Strange Constr), 734 Demaret Dr.

Bryson, Larry (associate circuit court judge), 3102 Rollingwood Dr.

Bulgin Development Co., 301 Vieux Carre Ct.

Bulgin, Lawrence & Jackie, (owner, Bulgin Development Co.), 810 E. Taylor St.

Burger King, 2015 W. Broadway

Burnette, Ray W. & Margaret A (constr worker, John Epple Constr Co), 208 St. Joseph St.

Byars, Theresa (social worker), 345 Washington Ave.

-C-

Call, Calvin (exec dir, Insurance Information Service), 564 Cowan Dr.

Calvary Baptist Church, 606 Ridgeway Ave.

Carnpbell, Charles C. & Penny A. (assoc provost, University), 811 Sycamore Lane

Carnpbell, Rex (prof. University, city council), 458 Forest Ave.

Carlson, Cass (mgr, C&C Constr Co.), 111 Deer Run Dr.

Carnes, Lloyd E (retired), 709 W. Sexton Rd.

Catlett, Richard, 2054 Lynnwood Dr.

Cave, John (ret circuit ct judge), Route 8

Central Bridge Co., Stadium Blvd. at West Broadway

Chinese Delicacies, 47 E. Broadway

Chou, David (owner, Chinese Delicacies) 47 E. Broadway

Coca-Cola Bottling Co, 1601 Business 63 S.

Commerce Bank, 500 Business Loop 70 W.

Community Rehabilitation Center, 1101 Hinkson Ave.

Conley, Frank (retired presiding judge, Springfield Co. Circuit Court), 200 Forum Blvd.

Country Kitchen, 1712 N. Providence Rd.

Covington, Mick (Police Dept.), 1001 Oak Lawn Dr.

Cowznofsky, Melvin (supt, Midway Hts School Dist), Route 3

Crawford, George E. & Jennie (pres, Crawford Const Co.), 2220 Shepard Blvd.

Crawford, George W. & Pearl L. (retired), 510 W. Worley St.

Crawford, William (retired), 344 Craig St.

Crowe, Albert, (electrician), 653 E. Walnut St.

Cullen, Barbara (sls associate, Action Realty), 1805A Stanford

-D-

D Sport Shop, 1034 E. Walnut St.

Daniel Boone Regional Library, 100 W. Broadway

David, Richard (phys), 255 Chapel Hill Rd.

Davis, Peter N. & Mary L. (prof, University), 700 S. Greenwood Ave.

Decker, David (principal, Ashland Elemen), Ashland

DeLann, Corlis (dir, Chautauqua Ctr), 222 Virginia Ave.

Dennison, David (student), 2712A Quail Dr.

Dersham, Watson W. & Rosalie W. (dir, Amer Heart Assn.), 604 W. Texas Ave.

Devine, James (prof, Univ), 2084 Lakeshore Dr.

Diekmann, John H. & Marilyn M. (asst mgr, Nowell's), 2605 Andy Dr.

Diver's Village, 131 S. 7th St.

Doak, David (asst public def), 303 West Blvd N.

Doelger, Mary J. (collection clrk, Orthopaedic Grp), 2305 Meadowlark Lane

Dooley, Kevin (veterinarian), Ashland

Downs, Cathy J. (student), 2401 W. Broadway, Apt. 119

Downtown Appliance Co., 1104 E. Broadway

Drexler, James S. & Vita A. (University extension), 2901 Burrwood Dr.

Drinnon, Deion (unemp), 312 N. Garth Ave.

Dueblar, Jan (voc. evaluator), 105 Albany, Apt. D

Duff, Ross (phys), 2302 Lynnwood Dr.

Durham, Weldon (chmn, univ. theater dept), 2004 Lynnwood Dr.

-E-

Easley, Blanche H. Mrs. (retired), 913 Sandifer Ave.

Egbert, Chris (Springfield police dept.), 608 Rock Quarry Rd.

Elder, William (retired), 2105 Rock Quarry Rd.

Ellis Fischel State Cancer Hospital, 115 Business Loop 70 W.

Elmore, Stuart (manager, North County grocery), 537 Benton St.

Enyart, Carl & Yolanda (t 3-M Co.), 3500 Vista Place

Estep, Glenda (secretary), 1005 N. Eighth St.

Estes, Jack & Wendy (mgr, Property Sales Inc.), 210 Sondra Ave.

Evers, Michael (unemp), 38 Colonial Village Trailer Ct.

Evers, Toris (waiter), 38 Colonial Village Trailer Ct.

Eye Care Associates, 909 University Ave.

-F-

Fahy, Dennis (student), 9 Business 63 S., Apt. 6

Fain, Daniel & Alida (mgr, Asphlund Tree Co.), 3718 Southridge Dr.

Fenton, Roy H. & Minerva S. (retired), 418 Sanford Ave.

Flenner, Lois (social worker), 234 S. Hitt St.

Forrester, Gene A. & Helen (pharmacist), 3390 Country Hill Ct.

Ficken, Sandra (Boone Hosp Ctr), 409 Vine St.

First National Bank & Trust Co., 801 E. Broadway

First Bank of Commerce, 8th and Cherry Streets

First Bank of Commerce East, 5 Business 63 S.

Fullington, A. & Juanita (repairman, Henderson Implement), 2704 Blue Ridge Rd.

-G-

G&D Steak House, 2001 W. Worley St.

Gantzer, Clark (assoc prof, Univ), 34 Oak Lawn

Gensicke, Mavis (emp, University), 1206 Haven Rd

Gentry, James K. & Mary Beth (prof, University), 1602 University Ave.

Gibbens, Chas G. & Jean (Credit Bureau), 3300 Westcreek Dr.

Gilliam, Arthur & Naomi (baker, Stephens College), 2708 Northridge Dr.

Glatz, Annette M. (sr acct clrk, University), 2212 Sunflower

Glenn, George (Columbia fire dept), 219 Limerick Lane

Gordon, Frank (USDA), 111 Dorsey St.

Gray, James (restaurant mgr), 211 Demaret Drive

Green, Richard (dir, parks and rec, City of Columbia), 342 Fredora Ave.

Green, William (instr, University), 208 Westwood

Gunter, Caryn M. (dir, Rape Crisis Ctr), 2004 W. Broadway, Apt. A

Gutreuter, Mary E. (lab technician), Route 2

-H-

Hagemann, Virginia P. (assoc prof, University), 1109 W. Stewart Rd.

Hamory, Bruce H. (asst prof, University), Route 1

Harris, Hugh S. Jr. (physicianr), 654 Canyon Dr.

Hartman, Gerald W. (realtor), 2100 W. Broadway

Hassler, George and Marie, 3456 Forum Blvd.

Hazard, I.R. & Edna M. (retired), 501 Hulen Dr.

Hedayati, Mohammed (student), 909 Providence Rd.

Heidy, John (police capt), 2167 Florida Court

Heinz, Cynthia E. (nurse), 1707 McAlester

Heinz, Timothy (dean, Univ), 2056 Hulen Dr.

Hickman High School, Bus. Loop 70 and Providence Road

Highbarger, Carroll W. (detective, Police Department), 310 Elm St.

Hines, Kenneth (asst chief, Boone Co. Fire Dist), 336 Walnut St.

Hinten, John & Sharon (emp Richards Assoc.), 2012 W. Ash St., Apt. 117

Hoffmaster, David (emp Stephens College), 21 N. Greenwood Ave.

Holt, J.O. (retired), 801 N. 8th St.

Hosmer, Craig (student), 303 Waugh St.

Hubbard, Clarry & Carolyn (students), 1614 Amelia St., Apt. 4B

Hughes, Ann (teacher), 1100 Mehl Rd., Apt. 1A

Hultz, Tamara (student), 2303 Whitegate Dr., Apt 3E

Hutton, Robert (city council), 909 Elm Grove Dr.

-I-

Installers Unlimited, 922 Business Loop 70 E.

Interstate 70 Shell, 1004 Stadium Blvd.

Interstate Pancake House, 1110 I-70 Dr. S W.

-J-

Jaeger, Roger D. & Marie A. (pres, House of Zenith), 1101 Hulen Dr.

Jeanne's Beauty Salon, 8 N. 2nd St.

Jeney, Agnes (cashier), 252 W. Brookside Lane

Jennings, Bill & Colleen M. (emp, Public Schools), 708 W. Texas Ave.

Johnson, Anne E. (technician), 8638 Argyle

Johnson, Walter (professor), 503 Edgewood Ave.

Johnston Audio Inc., 702 E. Broadway

Johnston, Charles (chancellor, Univ), Chancellor's Residence

Jones, Edward D. & Co., 907 E Broadway

Jones, Patrick (technician), 308 Oak St.

Jorgenson, Charles M. (artist), 15 Quaker Circle

-K-

KBIA Radio, 310 Jesse Hall, University

KCBJ-TV, Channel 17, 501 Business Loop 70 E.

KFRU Radio, 1911 Business Loop 70 E.

KOMU-TV, Channel 8, Highway 63 S.

Karins, Tom (telephone switchman), 4657 Southhampton

Karlin, Linda D. (social worker), 1417 Lexington Circle E.

Kamjanapun, Supit (student), 708A University Village

Kelley, Chris (Spfld. police dept.), 210 Harvard

Kelley Motor Spectrum, 500 Vandiver Drive.

Kelly, Chris S. (county clerk), 705 Glenwood Court

Kempf, Arleen (fiscal analyst, University), 306 W. Broadway

Kettle, Barry & Judy (insurance underwriter), 1700 Iris Dr.

Keyser, Robert D (student), 101 Green Meadows Rd., Apt. 101

Kidwell, Donald L. & S. Juanita (Eastgate Party Shop), 1117 Again St.

Knaebel, Alban F. (Hulett Heating), Route 3

Knipp Construction Co., 1204 Pannell St.

Knipp, Richard H. (Knipp Constr Co.), 210 Forest Ave.

Koenig, Richard E. & Corin (KCBJ-TV), addr unk

Kruse, Karl (stockbroker and city councilman), 2312 Cochero Ct.

Kruse, Linda (student), 201 N. Sixth St.

Krueger, Leon (prof, Univ), 3334 Rollins Rd.

Kuhlman, John M. (prof, University), Rt. 1, Hartsburg

-L-

Lamberti, Joseph W. & Ramona (prof, University), 1121 Woodhill Rd

Lang, David P. & Elizabeth S. (mgr, Subrogation Dept), 309 S. Glenwood Ave.

Law, Deborah (bank clerk), 211 E. Cherry St.

Lawhom, James E. (technician, City Electronics), 801 Schepker

Lear, Truman E. & Laura L. (retired), 1502 W. Ash St.

Lee, Richard L. (prof, University), Route 1

Legg, Phillip N. & Evelyn S. (retired), 1303 Parkridge Dr.

Lewis, Harry (teacher, Col. Public Schools), 211 Redbud Lane

Lindstrom, David D. (dir, University Y), 211 E. Glenwood Ave.

Loeppky, Richard (prof, of chemistry, University), 209 Hulen Dr.

Losty, Barbara (dean, Stephens College), 1026 Westwinds Ct.

Lucas, Lawrence W. and Emily (medical doctor), 210 Canterbury Dr.

Lusby, Earnestine (secretary, University), 300 W. Worley St.

Lynch, Sharon (nurse, city council), 21 11 E. Walnut St.

Lynn, Dale (mgr, Riddler Transportation), 311 E. Fourth St.

Lyon, Dianne (coach, Rock Bridge High School), 2411 Shepard Blvd.

-M-

Maddox, Gary (policeman), 1205 University Ave.

Malon, Richard (dir, water and light dept), 129 Colby Drive

Matthews, Rhoda F., 1406 Lynnwood

Mazzio's Pizza, 70 E. Broadway

McCrary, Marvin (police capt), 3100 Rollingwood Dr.

McDaniels, Edward (emp unk), 1305 Elleta Blvd.

McElyea, Ethel M. (retired), 107 W. Broadway

Mead, Larry E. & Kathleen P. (Editor, Sheep Breeder mag), 17 Bingham Rd.

Meade, Carol (student), 1011 S outhpark Dr., Apt. 4

Mermelstein, Albert H. & Joanne (emp Crippled Children's Clinic), 209 Sappington Dr.

Metz, John R. (teacher(, 203 Highland Circle

Milanek, Meghan (housewife), 3009 Lakeshore Dr.

Miller, Randall (asst mgr, Westlake's), 365 Terry Lane

Mitchell, Alice L. (retired), 2 E. Ridgeley Rd.

Mitchell, Herbert L. & Alice R. (emp, Center for Disabilities), 903 E. El Cortez Dr.

Mitchell, Wendell P. & Jeanette (policeman), 101 W. Texas Ave.

Monticelli, Stephen (Springfield police dept.), 2081 Bethel Rd.

Moore, Dennis (bank teller), 1315 Ashland Gravel Rd., Apt. G

Morse, Lowell (vice pres, MFA), 108 Forest Hill Ct.

Moseley, Joseph L. & Carol (county prosecutor), 1304 Woodhill Rd.

Mueller, Randy (State Purveyors), 856 Westwind Dr.

Muffay, Kay (co. treasurer), 303 Fleetwood Dr.

Murrin, Arthur W. & Colleen J. (fire eng, city), 1300 Dawn Ridge Rd.

Music Shop, 923 E. Broadway

Myers, Murry R. & Martha A. (Forum Cleaners), 810 Bourne Ave.

-N-

Nansen, James D. & Mary (doctor), 330 Bethel St.

Naugle Companies, Route 2, Box 138

Neal, Betty J. (sales, Sears), 203 Ruby Lane

Neal, Paul A. (police det.), 309 E. Rollins Rd.

Nelson, Roberta H. (secretary), 2001 Newton Dr.

New American Life Insurance Co., 3301 W. Broadway

Newberry, Dan (student), 205 College Ave.

Newhard Cook & Co., Brokers, 10 N. Garth Ave.

Nichols, John (switchman, tele co.) Route 2 Rocheport

Nicholson, Calvin (student), 101 Green Meadows Rd., Apt. 38

Ninnenger, Timothy & Bemadette (supply rep), Route 4

Noren, Wendy (county clerk), 3107 Blackberry Lane

Norgetown Laundry, Biscayne Mall

Novus Shop Inc., 22 S. 9th St.

Null, Mary Mrs. (retired), 1201 Paquin St., Apt. 707

-O-

Odor, Raymond W. & Carol A. (tchr-coach, schools), 2412 Bluff Blvd.

Olsen, Jennifer (sec), 4322 Georgetown Drive

Olson, Laura A. (nurse), 1203 Stone Court

Orange, Mark (deliveryman, Central Dairy), 805 Westwood Dr.

Orkin Terrnite & Pest Control, 1808 Vandiver

Oskins, Perry B. (prof, University), 1330 Overhill Rd.

Ousler, Cynthia (ret.), Senior Citizens Center

Owens, Kenneth & Debbie (city fire engr), Rt. 5, Box 344A

Oxenhandler, Brad (student), 8 Keene St., Apt. K71

-P-

Pa's Bait Shop, 1304 Wilkes Blvd.

Parsons, Douglas (Springfield police dept), 2016 Redbud Lane

Paulsell, Steve (chief, fire protection dist.), Route 5

Paulsen, Sandra (teacher, Hickman High), Route 3

Pelousky, John J. (unemployed),110 Hitt St.

Perez, Eli C. (analyst), 2302 Walther Court

Perkowski, Mitchell (University), 605 Fifth St., Apt. D.

Peterson, Mark (manager, Mazzio's Pizza), 3121 S. William St.

Phipps, Wendel (patrolman, Police Dept.), 613 Ninth St.

Pickering, Roger (laborer), 813 Rollingwood Dr.

Pitchford, June (co. auditor), 444 Fyfer Place

Poll, Max H. & Judith (adm, Boone Co. Hosp.), 1101 Lakeside Dr.

Posner, Mary, 3444 Grace Ellen Dr.

Powell, Albert (Central Electronics), 1206 Tandy Ave.

Pugh, Robert K. & Connie G. (vice pres, The Book Store), 502 W. Rock Creek Dr.

-R-

Rademacher, Cathy (Hairy's Place), 3500 N. Stadium Blvd.

Randell, Douglass (assoc prof, univ.), 2045 Bray Dr.

Rainey, Thomas G. (mgr Salty's Sandwiches), 1207 W. Ash St.

Rardin, J.E. & Associates, 213 Brewer Dr.

Ratliff, Earl D. & Lucille (retired), 511 Simmons Ct.

Rea, John (prof, University), 354 S. Wappel Dr.

Realty World, 1500 I-70 Dr. S.W.

Redman, Scott (emp unk), 1030 Southpark Dr., Apt. 2A

Reichenbacher, Barry R. & Martha S. (emp unk), 207 Pinewood Dr.

Regude, William, 902 Jefferson St.

Richards, Anna (housewife), 208 Thilly

Richter, Clifford (chief rad therapist, Ellis Fischel Hosp), 513 Woodridge Dr.

Ricks, Linda (clerk), Ashland

Rikli, Arthur E. & Frances M. (prof, University), 4003 Faurot Dr.

Ritter, James D. & Patty (assoc. schools supt.), 2190 Birch Road.

Robb's Kerr-McGee, 103 N. Providence Rd.

Roberts, C. David & Kristy (tchr, University), 1113 S. Glenwood Ave.

Robinson's Cleaners, 907 University Ave.

Rock Bridge High School, Providence Road

Rojanasuwan, Choochit (student), 413 Hitt St., Apt. 302

Roper, Ellen (judge, circuit court), 100 Fairway Drive

Rosenfeld, Harvey (rabbi, B'nai B'rith Hillel), 333 Crescent Rd.

Roshawn, William (emp, Masterhosts Inn), 1225 Elleta Blvd.

Ruffner, Robert (geologist), 710 Rogers St.

Rweter, Diana (aide, Woodhaven Leaming Ctr), Business 63 S.

Ryan, D. Charles (Morgan Crowe & Assoc), 818 Dogwood Ln

-S-

Sadich, Robert & Mary (dentist), 21 1 E. Danforth Dr.

Saiger, Paul & Linda (dir, B'nai B'rith Hillel Found.), 300 McNab Dr.

Samuels, William (atty), 2024 Lakeshore Dr.

Sanford, Michael R. & Marilyn K. (dir, dept. of community services), 3100 Hill Haven Lane

Schaeffer, Hal O. (student), 101 Green Meadows Rd., Apt. 13

Scheetz, Paul (Industrial and Petroleum Env. Serv), 2906 Weaver Dr.

Schneider, Dale and Cecilia, 316 Penny Lane

Schooley, Michael (principal, city schools), 2000 Weaver Dr.

Scott, Patricia (city clerk), 2110 West Blvd. S.

Sharp, Paul (prof, Univ), 2222 Shoreside

Scruggs, Vicki (secretary), 211 N. Eighth St.

Shern, Garland (farmer), Harrisburg

Shine, Jim (vice pres, Commerce Bank) 329 Frances Dr.

Shorter, David (student), 222 Sondra Ave.

Sievers, Dennis H. (prof, University), 773 Subella Dr.

Simpson, John R. (emp unk), 2703 Meadowlark Lane

Sletten, Craig (mgr, Iseman Mobile Homes), 3903 Clark Lane, Lot 123

Smeed, Nick (city personnel dir), 211 Lynnwood Dr.

Smith & Co., Inc., 16 E. Sixth St.

Smith, John (Ellis Fischel Hosp.), 909 Crawford

Smithton, Mohad (unemployed), 310 N. Tenth St.

Southwest Swim Club, 211 College Park Dr.

Spangler, Barrett (Burrito T-Shirt Co.), 1616 Radcliffe Dr

Stamper, Don (county court pres comm), Ashland

Stanley, Robert M. (lieutenant, fire dept.), 2401 W. Broadway

Stanton, Bobbi Sue (clerk), 1406 Lynnwood

Starrs, Robert L. Oanitor), 911 W. Sexton Rd.

Stephens, Steve M. (police sgt.), 1203 N. 9th St.

Stoerker, Lewis W. & Dorothy (state sec, Travelers Prot. Assn.), 106 College Ave.

Strawn, Estell P. (painting contr), 120 Pinewood Dr.

Stubben, Michael (Sheriff's Dept), 910 E. Oak St.

Sulzen, James D. & Lisa, 3900 Clark Lane, Lot 123

Swanson, Herbert C. Rev. & Chloe (Calvary Lutheran Church), 1914 Garden Dr.

Sylvester, Steve (student), 305 Edgewood Ave.

-T-

Taracido, Jorge (emp, University), 411 Parkade Blvd

Tarrant, Johnny L. & Loraine E. (chemist), 1401 Dawn Dr.

Taylor, Larry & Lee (law clerk), 4600 Oakview Dr.

Teter, Elizabeth (housemother), 600 E. Rollins St.

Thomann, David W. (student, University), 815 Cypress Lane

Thompson, Russell V. & Ruth (supt., city schools), Route 4

Thomiere, Nancy J. (emp Mental Health Ctr), 301 Tiger Lane, Apt. 208

Thompson, Nancy J. (bookkeeper, Adams Constr), Fulton

Thornburg, Jim (University emp), 234 S. Sixth St.

Tibbs, Joyce L. (clk Utilities Co.), 21 Sunset Trailer Ct.

Tillema, Herbert K. & Susan M. (assoc prof, University), 306 Westridge Dr.

Tolksdorf, Christina M. (student), 1405 Bouchelle Ave.

Touchstone, Michael (clerk), 307 Washington St.

Trautwein, Erwin L. & Mary H. (retired), 2 Miller Dr.

Tritschler, Ralph & Billie (construction worker), 2110 E. Cardinal Dr.

Turner, Charles S. & Anna L. (retired), 906 Charles St.

Turner, Shirley J. (custodian), Route 3

-U-

United Parcel Service, 2501 Vandiver Drive

United Way, Strollway Centre

University Y, 308 Read Hall

Urban, David L. & Leslie Ann (The Creative Eye), 2207 Bear Creek Dr.

-V-

VIP Travel Service, 101 W. Broadway

Valentine, A. Merrill & Juanita (Christman Jewelry), 111 Dawn Dr.

Veach, Dennis (police capt), 3711 Edison St.

Vining, Victor E. (supervisor, University), P.O. Box 219

Vogt, Christi N. (bank teller), 1509 Paris Rd

-W-

Wagahoff, Adeline (clerk), 1408 Parkade Blvd.

Wainscott, Richard (clerk, K mart), 333 Texas Ave.

Walkup, Starr A., 13 McBaine Ave.

Walls, Richard L. (Heidelberg restnt), 10 McGregor Lane

Walsh, David E. & Georgene (emp city), 27 E. Thurman St.

Walters, Robert (proj mgr, Highland Mgmt Properties), 333 Grace Ellen Dr.

Warren, David S. & Doris (computer analyst), 2 Comanche Ct.

Watkins, Paul A. & Rose T. (Paul Watkins Co.), 104 Off St.

Webber, Jonathan T. & Wendy (asst, University), 2221 Concordia St.

Welch, Sharron (dir, women studies, Univ), 206 S. Eighth St.

Wendy's Old Fashioned Hamburgers, 200 Business Loop 70 W.

Westlund, John D. & Janet L. (pres Real Estate Ctr), 2809 Biscayne Ct.

Wheeler, Douglas (sgt., Police Dept.), 308 Limerick Lane

Williams, John L., 805 Wilkes Blvd.

Willows, Jay & Peggy (dir, vocational education, public schools), 1214 N. Garth Ave.

Windmiller, Eugene & Perva L. (phys), 1502 E. Broadway

Windmiller, Myrl E. (firefighter), Route 1

Wood, Glenn (retired), 110 S. Garth Ave.

Woolford, Lyn (sheriff's deputy), 2110 W. Southpark Dr

Wright, Hewitt P. & Lynn A. (emp Amdahl Corp.), 900 Lynwood Ct.

Wright, Marvin E. & Janet (atty), 1109 Pheasant Run Dr.

Wu, Kung Yao (student), 1205 University Ave.

Wu, Shin (student), 1307 William St.

-Y-

Yaeger, Bob (D&H Enterprises), 2009 Wolcott Dr.

Yardley, Robert (unemp), 211 S. Fifth St.

Yates, Virgil T. & Janet B. (adm Ellis Fischel Hosp.), 1704 Princeton Dr.

Yeargin, Howard R. (carpenter), Route 9

Yeargin, Marge N. (emp unk), Route 7

Yeargin, Russell B. (salesman), 3435 E. William St.

Young, Millard (pub safety, Columbia Reg. Airport), 109 Woodside Dr.

Young, Toni D. (nurse, Boone Hospital Ctr), 100 Keene St., Apt. 10

Yowell, Ruby M. (retired), 902 Rogers St.

-Z-

Zimmerman, Roger (student), 3212 Woodbine

Zukowski, Marvin (optician), 311 Turner Ave.

Zwonitzer, Wilbur E. (building contractor), 1524 West Blvd. S.

Appendix IV
Springfield
Street Index

Springfield Street Index

-A-

Again Street
Alameda Court
Alan Lane
Aldeah Avenue
Alexander Avenue
Alfred Street
Alhambra Drive
Allen Street
Alsup Drive
Alton Avenue
Amelia Street
Ammonette Street
Anderson Avenue
Andy Drive
Ann Street
Anthony Street
Arapahoe Circle
Arapahoe Place
Arbor Drive
Argyle Road
Arlington Street
Ash Street
Ashland Gravel Road
Ashley Street
Aspen Drive
Aster Court
Atkins Drive
Auburn Lane
Audubon Drive
Austin Avenue
Aztec Boulevard

-B-

Balboa Lane
Ballenger Place
Ballenger Lane
Balow Wynd
Banks Avenue
Barberry Avenue
Barkley Avenue
Bass Avenue
Bayonne Court
Beachview Drive
Bear Creek Drive
Belle Meade Drive
Belleview Court
Belmont Street
Benton Street
Bernadette Drive
Berrywood Drive
Bethel Street
Bettina Drive
Beulah Drive
Beverly Drive
Bicknell Street
Big Bear Boulevard
Birch Road

Bingham Road
Biscayne Court
Bittersweet Court
Blackberry Lane
Blackfoot Road
Blair Court
Blossom Court
Blue Ridge Road
Bluff Boulevard
Bluff Dale Drive
Bob-O-Link Drive
Bonny Linn Drive
Bowling Street
Bouchelle Avenue
Bourn Avenue
Boyd Lane
Bradford Drive
Bradshaw Avenue
Braemore Road
Brandon Road
Bray Avenue
Brenda Lane
Brewer Drive
Brighton Street
Bristol Court
Broadhead Street
Broadway
Brookside Court
Brown's Station Rd.
Bruin Street
Bryant Street
Buckner Street
Bucks Run
Burlington Street
Burnam Avenue
Burnam Road
Burrwood Drive
Bushnell Drive

-C-

Calico Lane
Calvert Drive
Calvin Drive
Cambridge Drive
Camino Real
Caniff Circle
Canterbury Drive
Canyon Drive
Cardinal Drive
Carolyn Avenue
Carpenter Drive
Casa Circle
Cedar Cliff Drive
Cedar Lane
Chalmers Road
Chandler Court
Chantilly Court
Charles Street

Cherokee Lane
Cherry Street
Chestnut Street
Chickasaw Drive
Christian College
    Avenue
Circus Avenue
Clark Lane
Clarkson Road
Claudell Lane
Clayton Street
Cliff Drive
Clinkscales Road
Clinton Drive
Cochero Court
Coats Street
Colby Drive
Colgate
College Avenue
College Park Drive
Colonial Court
Colorado Avenue
Comanche Court
Concord Street
Concordia Drive
Condado Court
Conley Avenue
Conley Road
Cook Avenue
Cornell
Corte Hermoso
Corte Nuevo
Cosmos Place
Cottle Drive
Country Club Drive
Country Club Drive S.
Country Lane
Country Side Lane
Court Street
Coventry Lane
Covington Place
Cowan Drive
Craig Street
Crawford Street
Creasy Springs Road
Crescent Road
Crestland Avenue
Crestmere Avenue
Crestridge Drive
Crown Point
Crump Lane
Curtis Avenue
Cypress Lane

-D-

Dahlia Drive
Dakota Avenue
Danforth Circle

Danforth Court
Danforth Drive
Dartmouth
Davis Street
Dawn Ridge Road
Dean Street
Deer Run Drive
Defoe Court
Defoe Drive
Derek Court
Devine Court
Diamond Avenue
Dogwood Lane
Donnelly Avenue
Dorado Drive
Doris Drive
Dorsey Street
Dover Avenue
Duke Street
Duncan Street
Dundee Drive
Dysart Street

-E-

East Ash Street
East Boulevard
East Briarwood Lane
East Henley Drive
East Lexington Circle
East Parkway Drive
East Rockcreek Drive
East Sugar Tree
    Lane
East Walnut Street
East Willowbrook
    Road
Eastlake Drive
Eastland Circle
Eastwood Circle
Eastwood Drive
Edgewood Avenue
Edison Street
Edris Drive
Edwards Court
Eighth Street
El Cortez Drive
Eldorado Court
Eldorado Drive
Elleta Boulevard
Elliott Drive
Ellis Court
Elm Street
Elm Crove Drive
Elmview Drive
Essex Court
Eubank Court
Eugenia Street
Eva Drive

Evans Road
Evergreen Lane

-F-

Fair Haven Drive
Fair Lane
Fairmont
Fairview Avenue
Fairview Road
Fairway Drive
Falcon Drive
Faurot Drive
Fay Street
Fellows Drive
Fellows Place
Field Crest
Fifth Street
Fir Place
First Street
Fleetwood Drive
Flora Drive
Florence Avenue
Florida Court
Forest Avenue
Forest Hill Court
Fourth Street
Frances Drive
Fredora Avenue
Fulton Road
Fyfer Place

-G-

Garden Court
Garden Drive
Garnet Avenue
Garnet Drive
Garth Avenue
Gary Street
Gentry Avenue
George Court
Georgetown Drive
Gipson Court
Gipson Street
Glenn Drive
Glenwood Avenue
Glenwood Court
Glorietta Drive
Gordon Street
Grace Ellen Drive
Granada Boulevard
Grand Avenue
Grant Lane
Greeley Drive
Greeley Street
Greenwood Avenue
Greenwood Court
Green Meadows Road
Green Ridge Road

Green Valley Drive
Grindstone Avenue
Grissum Drive
Guitar Street

-H-
Haden Drive
Hamilton Way
Hardin Street
Hartley Court
Harvard
Hathman Place
Hatton Drive
Haven Road
Hawthorne Drive
Hazelwood Drive
Heather Lane
Heidman Road
Hendrix Drive
Henley Court
Heriford Road
Hickam Drive
Hickman Avenue
Hickory Hill Drive
Hickory Street
High Street
Highland Drive
Highridge Circle
Highridge Drive
Highview Avenue
Hill Haven Lane
Hillcrest Road
Hillside Drive
Hinkson Avenue
Hinkson Creek Road
Hirth Avenue
Hitt Street
Hodge Street
Holly Avenue
Hominy Branch
  Court
Honeysuckle Drive
Hope Place
Hubbell Drive
Hulen Drive
Hunt Avenue
Hunt Court

-I-
1-70 Drive N W.
1-70 Drive S.E.
I-70 Drive S.W.
Illingham Way
Illinois Avenue
Illinois Street
Independence Street
Indiana Avenue
Indiana Street
Industrial Drive
Ingleside Drive

Iowa Avenue
Iris Drive
Isherwood Circle
Isherwood Drive
Ivy Way

-J-
Jackson Street
Jake Lane
James Dale Road
Jean Rae Drive
Jefferson Street
Jewell Avenue
Joann Street
Johnson Drive
Jolene
June Lane
Juniper Court
Juniper Drive
Juniper Place

-K-
Kathy Drive
Keene Court
Keene Street
Kensington Road
Kentucky Boulevard
King Avenue
Knipp Street
Kohler Drive
Kraemer Court
Kuhlman Court

-L-
LaGrange Road
Lake of the Woods
  Road
Lake Street
Lakeshore Drive
Lakeside Drive
Lakeview Avenue
Lambeth Drive
Lamp Lane
Lancaster Drive
Lansing Avenue
Laoris Street
Larch Court
Lasalle Place
Lathrop Road
Laurel Drive
Lawrence Place
Lawnridge Court
Leawood Terrace
Lee Street
Leeway Drive
Lenoir Street
Leslie Lane
Lexington Court
Liberty Street
Lightview Drive

Lilac Drive
Lilly Court
Limerick Lane
Lindell Drive
Lindy Lane
Loch Lane
Locust Street
Loma Court
London Drive
Longfellow Lane
Longwell Drive
Lovejoy Lane
Lowe Street
Lowry Street
Luan Court
Lucas Way
Lucerne Court
Lynn Street
Lynnwood Drive
Lyon Street

-M-
McAlester Street
McBaine Avenue
McGregor Lane
McKee Street
Madera Drive
Madison Street
Madrid Lane
Magnolia Court
Malibu Court
Mallard Court
Manor Court
Manor Drive
Maplewood Drive
Marion Drive
Marsha Court
Martha Drive
Martin Drive
Mary Street
Marygene Street
Mary Jane Drive
Maryland Avenue
Marylee Drive
Matthews Street
Maupin Road
Meadow Lane
Meadowlark Lane
Meadowvale Court
Medavista Drive
Mehl Road
Melbourne Street
Melody Lane
Mesa Drive
Mexico Gravel Road
Middlebush Drive
Mikel Street
Milibrook Drive
Mimosa Court
Miramar Lane

Mission Court
Missouri Avenue
Mitchell Court
Mohawk Avenue
Mohawk Court
Monroe Street
Monterey Drive
Moon Valley Road
Morning Glory Drive
Moss Street
Mt. Vernon Avenue
Mulberry Road
Mumford Drive
Murrell Drive

-N-
Navaho Avenue
Nebraska Avenue
Nelwood Drive
New Haven Avenue
Newton Drive
Nichols Street
Nifong Boulevard
Ninth Street
Noble Court
Norma Court
North Boulevard
North Circle
Northridge Drive
North Parklawn
  Court
North Valley View
  Drive
North Wappel Drive
Northland Drive

-O-
Oak Forest Drive
Oak Lawn Drive
Oak Street
Oakhaven Drive
Oakland Gravel
  Road
Oakland Place
Oakview Drive
Oakwood Court
Oakwood Drive
Olive Street
Onofrio Court
Orange Street
Orchard Court
Orchard Lane
Oriole Lane
Orleans Court
Orr Street
Otto Court
Overhill Court
Overhill Road
Oxford
Oyama Street

-P-
Pannell Street
Paris Court
Paris Road
Park Avenue
Park DeVille Drive
Park Hill Avenue
Parkade Boulevard
Parker Street
Parklawn Court
Parklawn Drive
Parkridge Court
Parkridge Drive
Parkside Drive
Parkview Drive
Paseo Hennoso
Patsy Lane
Paquin Street
Pearl Avenue
Pecan Street
Pendleton Street
Pennant Street
Pennsylvania Drive
Perkins Drive
Pershing Road
Petite Court
Pheasant Run Drive
Phyllis Avenue
Pickford Place
Pierre Street
Pin Oak Court
Pine Drive
Pinecrest Drive
Pinewood Drive
Pioneer Drive
Planter Road
Plaza Drive
Pleasant Way
Plymouth Drive
Ponderosa Street
Poplar Street
Porter Street
Powell Drive
Powell Lane
Pratt Street
Price Avenue
Primrose Drive
Princeton Drive
Proctor Drive
Prospect Street
Providence Road

-Q-
Quail Drive
Queen Ann Drive
Quisenberry Drive

-R-
Radcliffe Drive
Randy Lane

Range Line Street
Readosa Lane
Red Oak Lane
Redbud Lane
Redwood Road
Rhonda Lane
Riback Road
Rice Road
Richardson Street
Richland Road
Richmond Avenue
Rider Avenue
Ridge Road
Ridgefield Road
Ridgeley Road
Ridgemont
Ridgemont Court
Ridgeway Avenue
Riney Lane
Ripley Street
Riviera Drive
Robert Ray Court
Robert Ray Drive
Rock Quarry Road
Rock Wood Place
Rockhamton Circle
Rockhill Road
Rockingham Drive
Rogers Street
Rollingwood Drive
Rollins Road
Rollins Street
Roosevelt Avenue
Rose Cliff Drive
Rose Court
Rose Drive
Rosemary Lane
Ross Street
Rothwell Drive
Rowe Lane
Rowland Road
Ruby Lane
Russell Boulevard
Rustic Road
Rutledge Drive
Rye Lane

-S-
St. Andrew Street
St. Ann Court
St. Charles Road
St. Christopher

Street
St. James Street
St. Joseph Street
St. Michael Drive
Sandifer Avenue
Sanford Avenue
Sanford Street
Santiago Drive
Sappington Drive
Schwabe Lane
Scott Boulevard
Sears Court
Second Street
Seneca Avenue
Seventh Street
Seville Avenue
Sexton Road
Seymour Road
Shannon Place
Shepard Boulevard
Shepard Court
Sherwood Drive
Sheryl Drive
Shockley Street
Short Street
Sierra Madre
Silvey Street
Simmons Court
Sims Street
Sinclair Street
Sixth Street
Skye Wynd
Skylark Drive
Skyview Road
Smarr Court
Smiley Lane
Smith Street
Sondra Avenue
South Country Club
   Drive
South Drive
South Fastwood
Circle
South Wappel Drive
Southhampton Drive
Southpark Drive
Southridge Drive
Southwood Drive
Spencer Avenue
Spring Hill Road
Spring Valley Road
Spruce Drive

Squire Circle
Stadium Boulevard
Stalcup Street
Stanford Drive
Starke Avenue
Starlight Drive
Stephen Drive
Stevendave Drive
Stewart Road
Stone Street
Stoney Lane
Stony Brook Place
Strawn Road
Subella Drive
Summit Road
Sunflower Street
Sunset Drive
Sunset Lane
Surfside Court
Switzler Street
Sycamore Lane
Sylvan Lane

-T-
Taft Street
Tahoe Court
Tammy Lane
Tandy Avenue
Tara Lane
Taylor Street
Teal Drive
Tejon Circle
Tenth Street
Terry Lane
Texas Avenue
Thilly Avenue
Third Avenue
Thistledown Drive
Thornhill Road
Thurman Street
Tiger Lane
Timber Hill Road
Timber Hill Trail
Tipton Terrace
Topaz Drive
Towne Drive
Tracy Drive
Tremaine Drive
Trinity Place
Troyer Drive

Truman Drive
Tulip Court
Tupelo Place
Turner Avenue
Turner Drive
Twin Oak Court
Twin Oak Drive

-U-
University Avenue

-V-
Valencia Drive
Valley Court
Valley View Road
Vandiver Drive
Vassar
Vegas Drive
Victoria Drive
Vine Street
Violet Court
Virginia Avenue
Vista Place

-W-
Wabash Drive
Waco Road
Walcox Drive
Wales
Wallace Street
Walnut Suwt
Walther Court
Warwick Street
Washington Avenue
Waterford Court
Waterford Drive
Waterloo Drive
Watson Place
Waugh Street
Wayne Road
Wayside Drive
Wee Wynd
West Boulevard
   Court
West Boulevard
   North
West Boulevard
   South
West Briarwood Lane
West Henley Drive
West Lexington
   Circle

West Parkway Drive
West Rockcreek
   Drive
West Sugar Tree
   Lane
West Walnut Court
Westmount Avenue
Westover Street
Westport Drive
Westridge Drive
Westwind Drive
Westwinds Court
Westwinds Drive
Westwood Avenue
Weymeyer Drive
Wheaton Court
White Gate Drive
White Oak Lane
Wilde Drive
Wilkes Boulevard
Will Lane
William Street
Willis Avenue
Willow Way
Willowbrook Court
Wilson Avenue
Windmill Court
Windsor Street
Wolfcreek Court
Wood Ilill Road
Woodbine Drive
Woodkirk Lane
Woodland Drive
Woodlawn Avenue
Woodlea Drive
Woodrail Avenue
Woodrail Terrace
Woodridge Court
Woodridge Drive
Woodridge Road
Woodrow Street
Woods Court
Woodside Drive
Woodson Way
Worley Street
Wyatt Lane
Wyoming Avenue

-Y-
Yale
Yorktown Drive
Yuma Drive

Appendix V
Page-Design
Specifications

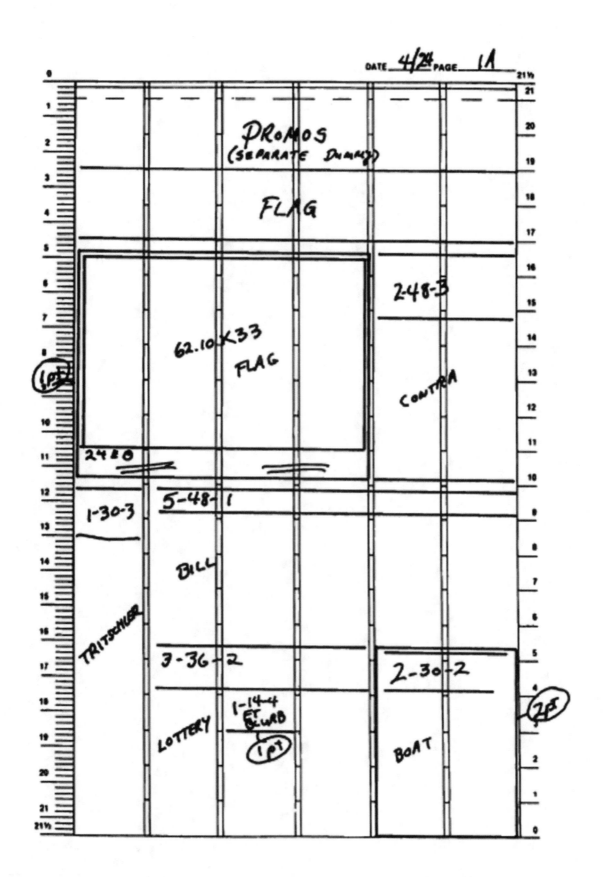

Dutch touch

That's a winner

Is Coke still it?

The Daily Constitution

Senate passes, House defeats contra aid plan

Groundwork

Tritschler wins nod by one vote

Bill would give M.U. $240 million plus

Compromise lottery bill's fate hinges on taxation of winnings

The bill's sponsor, Sen. Ed Dirck, D-St. Louis, doesn't want winnings taxed.

Japanese fishing boat seized by Soviet vessel

295

Understanding the Math of Page Design

PAGE DIMENSIONS

The page dummy forms in this workbook are drawn to scale to correspond with a standard six-column format. Columns are 12 picas, two points in width, and gutters are one pica (12 points). In the charts in this appendix, standard settings for such a page are listed. Numbers following decimal points are expressed in points, not tenths, so the base unit is 12, not 10. For example, 12.10 picas would not be the same as 13 picas. Instead, it would be two points narrower than 13 picas. Expressed another way, 12.10 picas plus 12.10 picas would equal 25.8 picas.

GUTTER-TO-GUTTER COLUMN WIDTHS

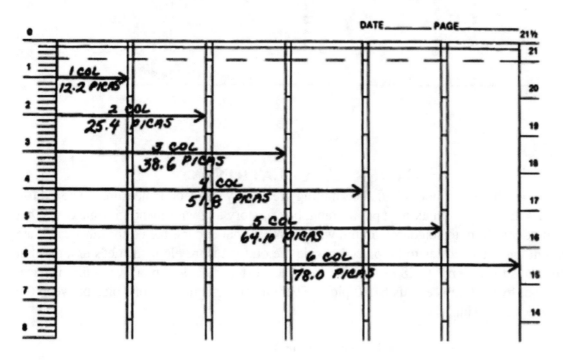

These measurements allow the editor to determine the exact width of photographs in picas and points. Thus, a three-column photo would be 38.6 picas wide. Knowing that measurement allows the editor to calculate the exact depth of the photo once it is sized for publication. This is essential in page design.

Understanding the gutter-to-gutter dimension system also allows the editor to make exact calculations for odd-measure settings of stories. Assuming that all gutters, even those between type wraps in boxed stories, are to remain at one pica, and assuming that one pica is needed on each side of the box to allow for the rule, such calculations are made simple. To eliminate the need to calculate the measure each time, these charts will serve as a handy reference guide:

297

Number of Type Wraps	Number of Columns	Setting
1	1	12.2
1	2	25.4
2	3	18.9
3	4	16.7
4	5	15.5
5	6	14.10

Note: Other combinations, such as three measures in five columns, are possible. That, however, would produce a setting of 21.1 picas, and anything in excess of 20 picas generally is considered too wide for easy legibility of newspaper text type.

ODD MEASURES (Boxed Stories)

Number of Type Wraps	Number of Columns	Setting
1	1	10.2
2	2	11.2
2	3	17.10
3	4	15.11
4	5	14.11
6	6	14.5

OTHER CALCULATIONS

The preceding charts are helpful in determining frequently used odd measures. The editor, however, has the option of making a photograph, box or story any width, and in some cases that width will not conform to standard column widths. When that occurs, the editor must calculate the type setting of the stories to be placed beside the odd-measure element. Let's assume that the editor plans to run a photo 28 picas wide and place a story beside it in a five-column space. We know that five columns equals 64.10 picas. There must be a gutter of one pica between the photo and the story. Thus:

$$
\begin{array}{ll}
64.10 & \text{(five columns)} \\
-28.0 & \text{(photo width)} \\
\hline
36.10 & \\
-\ 1.0 & \text{(gutter)} \\
\hline
35.10 & \text{(space for type)}
\end{array}
$$

We know that type should not be set 35.10 picas wide, so two wraps of type are necessary. That means another gutter (the one between the two legs of type) will be needed:

$$
\begin{array}{ll}
35.10 & \\
-\ 1.0 & \text{(second gutter)} \\
\hline
34.10 & \text{(space left for type)} \\
\div\ 2.0 & \text{(number of wraps of type)} \\
\hline
17.5 & \text{(type setting for story)}
\end{array}
$$

298

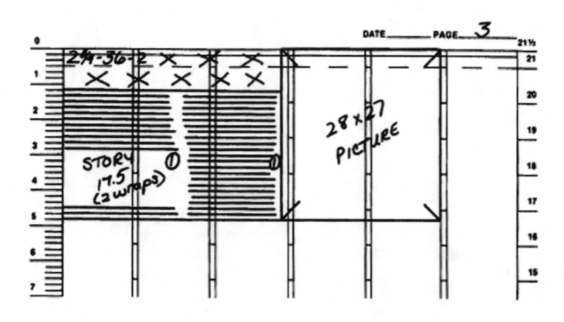

CUTLINE WIDTHS

Because cutlines, or photo captions are frequently set larger than body type, and because they are brief, their width may exceed 20 picas. Here is a handy chart for determining cutline settings in our standard page format:

Column Width	Number of Wraps	Setting
1	1	12.2
2	1	25.4
3	2	18.9
4	2	25.4
5	2	31.11
6	3	25.4

Cutline settings for boxed or odd-measure photographs would have to be calculated using the system outlined earlier.

CALCULATING STORY LENGTHS

Editors with computers have no trouble calculating story lengths; the computer does it for them. Editors who deal with typewritten copy must judge the length of a story before it is typeset. Typically, three typewritten lines of copy will produce about one column inch of type set 12.2 picas wide.

NOTES

NOTES

NOTES